New Georgia pattern for victory

D C Horton

Pan/Ballantine

Editor-in-Chief: Barrie Pitt
Editor: David Mason
Art Director: Sarah Kingham
Picture Editor: Robert Hunt
Designer: Michael Frost
Cover: Denis Piper
Special Drawings: John Batchelor
Photographic Research: Jonathan Moore
Cartographer: Richard Natkiel

Photographs for this book were specially selected from the following Archives: from left to right page 4–5 US Army; 9 US Marine Corps; 10 Australian War Memorial; 11 US National Archives; 11 US Army; 14 US Airforce; 15 US Marine Corps; 16–17 Keystone; 18 US Marine Corps; 18 US Airforce; 19 US Marine Corps; 20 US Army; 20–23 US Nat Arch; 26–27 US Marine Corps; 30 US Navy; 31 US Army; 33 Imperial War Museum; 36–42 US Nat Arch; 43 US Army; 45–47 US Marine Corps; 50 US Marine Corps; 50–56 US Nat Arch; 56–60 US Marine Corps; 64 US Army; 64 US Nat Arch; 65–66 US Army; 68 US Nat Arch; 71 US Army; 72 US Marine Corps; 73–76 US Army; 77 US Nat Arch; 80 US Marine; 80 US Nat Arch; 83 US Airforce; 84–87 US Nat Arch; 89 US Army; 92–93 US Marine; 94 US Army; 94 US Nat Arch; 97 US Army; 100–102 US Army; 103 US Marine; 106–7 US Marine; 108 US Army; 111 US Nat Arch; 114–117 US Nat Arch; 119 US Army; 120 IWM; 121 US Marine; 126–127 US Army; 128 US Marine; 131 US Nat Arch; 132 IWM; 133–134 US Nat Arch; 136–137 US Army; 138 US Nat Arch; 139 US Army; 139 US Nat Arch; 140–141 US Airforce; 143 US Marine; 144 US Nat Arch; 145–155 US Marine; 157–159 US Army; Front cover US Army; Back cover US Army

First U.S. Printing: July, 1971
First Pan/Ballantine Printing: August, 1972

Printed in the United States of America
Ballantine Books, Ltd.—An Intertext Publisher
Pan Books, Ltd.
33 Tothill Street, London, S.W. 1

Contents

A tale of courage

In an explosion of military energy which riveted the attention of the world from December 1941 and on through the following six months, the Japanese inflicted crushing defeats on all who stood in their way. In Malaya, Singapore and Hong Kong they cost the British over 150,000 casualties; in the Dutch East Indies their furious onslaught killed, wounded or captured over 75,000 British, American and Dutch, while in the Philippines they virtually obliterated a force of over 100,000 American and Filipino troops. From the British they took Singapore and from the Americans Corregidor – despite the fact that their attacking forces were numerically smaller than those of the defenders. But they were well-trained and united whereas their opponents were confused and disorganized; and to those opponents, as Japanese victory followed Japanese victory, the conquerors appeared well-nigh invincible.

But with the Battle of Midway in June 1942 the picture was changed, for here the Americans inflicted on the Japanese what has been called 'a cataclysmic blow', wiping out Japanese superiority in naval air strength – and in the prosecution of the war in the Pacific this was to prove the key factor. Although Midway did not mark the end of Allied defeats, it was in fact the turning of the tide; the high water mark of Japanese military achievement had been reached, and from now on success would come more and more often to Allied arms.

It was to be, nonetheless, a hard-won success and at the beginning almost imperceptible, for the Allies were pitted against an enemy whose conquests had been made swiftly and cheaply and who was now poised, armed and alert, to defend those conquests against all counteraction. For the Allies, therefore, the way back would be long and hard.

In August 1942 the first tottering step on the uphill path of reconquest was made. US Marines went ashore on Guadalcanal and some tiny neighbouring islands to begin a six month calvary of bitter fighting. Starting with near disaster – for all attempts at recovering lost territory tend to be made by hastily formed bodies of partially trained troops – the campaign demonstrated that successful operations in the Pacific would demand co-operation between services and that pre-war prejudices must be cast aside.

After the completion of the Guadalcanal campaign, which had added such an illustrious chapter to the Marine Corps history, the second phase in the New Britain/New Ireland/New Guinea area plan was started – the invasion of the Central Solomons which is the subject of this book. D C Horton gives a lucid account of the operations which took place between June and October 1943, from Operation Toenails – the invasion of New Georgia Island – to Operations Goodtime and Blissful against Mono and Choiseul respectively; he also describes the stepping-stone operation – Cleanslate – mounted from Cape Esperance, Guadalcanal in February 1943 which secured the Russel Islands for the Allies.

The activities of that remarkable organization, the Solomon Islands Coastwatchers, figure largely in this book because of the important part they played in ensuring that the Allies were always informed of Japanese moves as soon as they took place; the Coastwatchers also acted as contacts for specialist patrols sent out to obtain vital terrain and hydrographic information without which future landings would be made more dangerous. So important was this band of brave and dedicated men, that Admiral Halsey later wrote of them that 'he never made a forward move without their help' in the Solomons campaign.

D C Horton was himself a Coastwatcher, living in enemy-occupied territory, sending in his regular and invaluable intelligence reports, and when parties were being sent from Guadalcanal to reconnoitre the Central Solomons, he provided scouts from among his helpers on Rendova Island.

Not surprisingly, therefore, he writes with admiration and affection of the Solomon Islanders with whom he lived and worked. These men fought the Japanese in the bush they knew so well, becoming particularly adept in the art of ambush – so much so that the Japanese were forced to increase the size of their patrols considerably as small patrols seldom returned to base. The Islanders also operated a highly efficient recovery organization for Allied servicemen stranded in the Solomons – shot-down fliers or naval survivors – whom they shepherded to the nearest Coastwatcher under the very noses of the enemy, for a pick-up to be arranged by radio. One such survivor was Lieutenant John F Kennedy, later President Kennedy, whose PT boat had been run down and sunk by the Japanese destroyer *Amagiri* in a night action in the Slot off Kolombangara.

Throughout, however, the Japanese defenders fought with fanatical courage; as General Slim later wrote, 'We all talk of fighting to the last man and the last bullet, the Japanese soldier was the only one who did it'. On New Georgia they were well-ensconced in log-and-coral bunkers from which they had to be burned and blasted, and when surrounded in the Kokenggolo Hills they took to the caves beneath them and refused to surrender. Eventually the entrances were dynamited and the occupants entombed underground.

Thus, D C Horton's fascinating narrative deals in large part with people of non-Western racial origin – and it is a narrative full of a degree of courage which the West has often arrogantly assumed to be chiefly a Western quality.

It is as well to remember that courage is, in fact, universal.

Introduction by Barrie Pitt

Attack on the Central Solomons

The Solomon Islands were formed by a crinkling of the bed of the Pacific ocean some 2,000,000,000 years ago and consist of six major islands and many smaller ones. They are nearly all of volcanic origin and stretch some 1,000 miles north west to south east from the Shortland Islands south east of Bougainville in the Australian mandated territory of Papua-New Guinea, to the small outlying island of Fataka in the Santa Cruz group, which itself is to the north of the Torres and Banks islands in the condominium of New Hebrides. North to south from the atoll of Ontong Java (the largest in the world) to the upthrown coral atolls which are the islands of Rennell and Bellona is about 500 miles and the total land area of the Solomons is about 11,500 square miles. On the map they lie between meridians 156 and 170 and Latitudes 6 and 13 South.

The precise origin of the people of the Solomons is unknown. They are probably the descendants of migrating tribes which came from the Indo Caucasus eastwards and were joined by people from the mainland of China moving southwards. These streams of wanderers spread through the archipelago of Indonesia and came eventually via Papua and New Guinea to the Solomons. They came in waves and it is thought that the first inhabitants of the islands established themselves about 50 BC but there was no continuity of tribe and language and each island has a different people on it and the dialects on each island are such that no one dialect will carry the speaker very far. This situation has been resolved by the use of 'pidgin English' as the lingua franca throughout the Solomons, although English is gradually replacing the picturesque, forceful but inelastic 'pidgin'.

The majority of the people belong to the Melanesian race which is closely linked with Papuasian stock. The individuals of this race are sturdy people averaging about five feet, three

US Marines and islanders move inshore

Above: RAAF Catalinas remain at Gavatu island. *Below:* The Coastwatchers. With the help of these men and their native spies and saboteurs the campaign is greatly shortened and casualties reduced

Admiral Ernest J King

General Douglas MacArthur

inches in height; their skins vary from black to a light brown and their features are generally of a negroid cast. The Polynesians on the other hand, who form the second largest component, have straight hair, light brown skins and are taller in stature. They came to the Solomons from the islands of the central Pacific and their ancestors occupied the outlying islands and atolls. Indeed their occupation of the islands of Rennell and Bellona marked the furthest westwards point reached by the Polynesians in the Pacific. At the time of the invasion of the Solomons in 1942 the population was approximately 100,000 people of all races.

The Solomons were discovered by Alvaro de Mendana in February 1568. He had sailed westwards from Peru and returned there with the remains of his expedition in September 1569. He returned to the islands in 1595 with the intention of colonising them but the expedition ended in disaster and two surviving ships eventually reached the Phillipines. The islands were 'lost' for some years and it was not until 1643 that they were rediscovered by Abel Tasman. Various expeditions visited them subsequently and as time went on European traders

and planters began to settle there despite the fierce and warlike inhabitants who were notorious for their cannibalistic practices, and in January 1893 the British Government declared a Protectorate over the islands and C M Woodford was appointed first Resident Commissioner in 1896.

The 1914-1918 war had little effect on the islands, which saw no fighting, and subsequently they remained as a small, very isolated, self supporting Colonial Dependency of which few people had ever heard and which was only of interest to the small group of European inhabitants engaged in administration, mission activities, trading and the production of copra. The government was centred on the small island of Tulagi lying off the larger island of Ngela and the administrative control of the Protectorate was vested in eight districts in charge of District Officers. The situation had not changed at the outbreak of war in 1939 and after initial activity the islands returned to their peace for a year or so until it became clear that the Japanese, who were advancing triumphantly southwards, would invade the islands which lay directly across their path. There was nothing

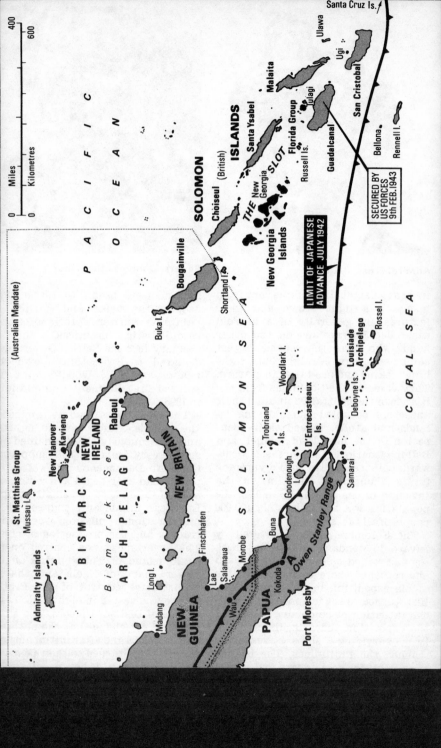

to stop them. The forces which might have done so were fighting in the Middle East and all that remained was an RAAF Catalina reconnaissance squadron based on Gavutu Island in Port Purvis south east of Tulagi, a platoon of the AIF Independent Company to guard them, the District Administration, missionaries and a few traders who had decided to remain and the branch of the Royal Australian Navy known as 'The Coastwatchers'. The Japanese invaded the northern Solomons in April 1942 and the RAAF Squadron and their guard platoon withdrew as ordered after destroying all installations leaving nothing between the Japanese and the islands to the south east except the District Officers under the direction of the Resident Commissioner and the Intelligence network of the Coastwatchers.

The progress of the Japanese southwards had been causing concern to the Allies but there were two schools of thought on the matter. General Marshall was of the opinion that the war in Europe should come first and that the Japanese should be dealt with

after that. Admiral King and General MacArthur saw the matter as much more urgent. The swift Japanese advance was going to cut the Allied life line to Australia and New Zealand and there was little time left to halt them. It was imperative to stop them as soon as possible. This view prevailed and it was decided to use the United States Marine Corps as the initial force with which to oppose the Japanese, and to follow up their attack with army units.

The overall strategy of the war in the Pacific envisaged first the halting of the Japanese advance and second, an Allied attack toward Japan using the islands lying to the south and south east of that country as stepping stones. This strategical approach was modified later but the initial plan was successful and the Allied forces landed on Guadalcanal and Tulagi on 7th August 1942. There followed months of bitter fighting until, in Feburary 1943, the Japanese had been driven off Guadalcanal. The Allied plan then called for the pursuit of the Japanese northward in order to seize their bases en route to their key base of Rabaul. The Japanese had invaded and taken Rabaul on 23rd January 1942, as they had long realised its exceptional

Rabaul, main Japanese base in the South-West Pacific

importance in dominating the area to the south east which they intended to invade.

Rabaul is situated on the extreme north east tip of New Britain island on the shore of Simpson harbour, 436 miles from Port Moresby in Papua and 570 miles from Guadalcanal, thus providing an excellent position from which to dominate the northern coast of New Guinea, the Bismarck Archipelago, the chain of the Solomons and the surrounding seas. By May 1942, Rabaul had replaced Truk in the Caroline Islands as the Japanese citadel in the Pacific.

After Guadalcanal had been conquered the Japanese had withdrawn to the islands in the Central Solomons and their largest base was at Munda on New Georgia. The islands in this area lie between meridians 156 and 158 and comprise the large islands of New Georgia, Kolombangara, Vella Lavella, Ganongga, Rendova, Tetepari, Gatukai, Vangunu and many smaller islands. The approximate centre of the group is at Munda point which is on the south west tip of New Georgia island and about 170 miles west north west of Tulagi and Guadalcanal with the small group known as the Russell Islands some 125 miles to the south

east acting as a stepping stone between New Georgia and Guadalcanal. The Russells have soil which is particularly suitable for coconut growing and the greater part of them is covered with plantations. The terrain of the islands in the central Solomons, like that of the other islands, is very rugged with heavy rain forest covering their volcanic cores. There are no roads except a type of coral track on some plantations and the few paths follow the coast or go inland to gardens over razor backed coral ridges. The jungle growth is lush and very difficult to penetrate while the shores have many mangrove filled inlets alive with mosquitos.

Offshore lie lagoons fringed with coral reefs; the Marovo lagoon on the north coast of New Georgia stretches the length of the island and is the largest lagoon in the world. On the south coast the Roviana lagoon stretches some thirty miles to the east and west varying in width from one to three miles. South of it across the Blanche channel Rendova island lies $7\frac{1}{2}$ miles away and its dog leg shape has reefs on the north shore enclosing the

Marines pause in a jungle clearing en route the front on Guadalcanal

waters of Renard Sound above which a mountain rises to 3,488 feet amongst the clouds. Tetepari island which is nearly flat and largely covered by a coconut plantation lies to the south east of Rendova. Vangunu and Gatukai are to the south east of New Georgia while Kolombangara and Vella Lavella stretch north west of it separated from New Georgia by the Kula and Vella gulfs with Arundel Island to the south of Kula Gulf and Gizo and Ganongga islands closing off Vella Gulf at its southern end.

The coastlines of the New Georgia group are irregular and some of the larger inlets, notably Rice Anchorage, Bairoko Harbour, Enogai, Sunday Inlet and the Diamond Narrows on the New Georgia shore of the Kula Gulf, form anchorages for vessels of some size. It was over this very difficult terrain and in and around the large islands, the lagoons, inlets, small

Former cannibals train hard to defend their island against the invading Japanese

islands and channels that the battles for the Central Solomons took place between 24th June 1943 – when half the 4th Marine Raider Battalion landed at Segi Point, the Headquarters of Major D G Kennedy, DSO, District Officer and Coastwatcher in that area – and the 9th October 1943, when the 3rd New Zealand Division declared the island of Vella Lavella secure. The fighting on Guadalcanal had been intense and fierce but in the Central Solomons it was, if anything, of far greater range in its violence and variety.

As a result of the battle for Guadalcanal between 7th August 1942 and 8th February 1943 the Japanese drive towards New Zealand and Australia had been stopped and the Japanese left on Guadalcanal had been evacuated to their base on New Georgia. The Allies had begun to build up a formidable mass of men and material aided by their superiority in communications and the enormous industrial complex which was able to outstrip the production of the Japanese. Apart from these the Allies

had several other advantages. First, the people of the Solomons had given and continued to give full and steadfast support to the Allies and were under administrative control, and wherever they went the Allied forces could count on the complete cooperation of the Solomon Islanders whereas the Japanese were detested. Second, the Allies had won the first battle in the campaign and third, the Allied commanders were never unaware of the movements of the enemy.

This last and most important factor was the result of the activities of the Coastwatchers, that section of the Royal Australian Naval Intelligence Division whose men, from positions behind and within Japanese held areas provided a constant, accurate and rapid stream of information for the Allied Commanders in the field. The Coastwatching organisation had been set up immediately after the First World War, in 1919, at the suggestion of Captain C J Clare, CMG, ADC, RAN, the District Naval Officer, Western Australia. Selected individuals in the coastal areas of Australia and the territories for which Australia was responsible together with the British Solomon Islands Protectorate were organised to report any unusual or suspicious happenings particularly of shipping and aircraft. At the outbreak of the Second World War those not already in the services were enrolled and all activities were intensified. Teleradios with a range of 500 miles on voice and twice that range on morse key had been provided and throughout the islands to the north and east of Australia the communication network functioned actively and efficiently. Commander R B M Long, OBE, RAN, the Director of Naval Intelligence, directed the overall activities of the organisation whose code name in the islands was 'Ferdinand' and Commander E A Feldt, OBE, RAN, directed Ferdinand activities in the field. The headquarters of the Solomon Islands division was on Guadalcanal under the command of Lieutenant-Commander H Mackenzie, Legion of Merit, RAN.

Sergeant Major Vouza, scarred hero of
the Solomon Islands Constabulary

Lieutenant-General Harmon, army
troops commander in the South Pacific

Munda airfield, Rendova Island in background

From the inception of the campaign in 1942 he had foreseen the vital importance of having Coastwatchers in areas behind the Japanese lines covering all the sea and air approaches to Guadalcanal. Consequently, when the Allied invasion of New Georgia and the other islands of the Central Solomons was being planned it had the advantage of a constant stream of Intelligence, air and sea raid warnings from the Coastwatchers already in place on Bougainville, Choiseul, New Georgia, Vella Lavella Kolombangara and Rendova islands. The Coastwatchers and their guerilla organisation, together with the very active co-operation of the local people, reported on targets, rescued Allied pilots and seamen, and sabotaged and generally harassed the enemy. None of these activities would have been possible without the bravery and loyalty of the Solomon Islanders which was outstanding throughout the war. Sergeant-Major Vouza of the Solomon Islands Defence Force who was awarded the George Medal for outstanding courage and devotion to duty while under torture by the Japanese, put it simply: 'I remember my training in the Police . . . so I tell myself that this time I do something good for my King . . .'

Both sides had learned to respect the fighting qualities of their adversaries during the struggle for Guadalcanal, and in the fighting for New Georgia and the Central Solomons the Japanese would not again be taken by surprise nor would the Allies underestimate what would be required in terms of men and material to subdue a stubborn, courageous and hard fighting enemy. In fact the battle would be a slugging match and the side which could provide the greatest number of men and amount of material in the area of the fighting most quickly would win.

Both sides had learned to their cost that shipping could only proceed safely under an air umbrella and Allied planning was based on the distances which could be covered by aircraft operating from land bases since aircraft carrier operations were vulnerable and of necessity of short duration. There were three considerations which led to the choice of New Georgia as the next Japanese held base to be captured. The first was that New Guinea and its surrounding

Troops land from inflatable boats on Russell Island

Above: Supplies build up on Yellow Beach, Banika. *Below:* Two SBDs take off from an airstrip in the Russell Islands

islands lay within the radius of air cover for the troops on the ground; the second was that Allied shipping subject to surface attack could retire to the safety of Tulugi and Guadalcanal; the third was that the airstrip constructed by the Japanese garrison at Munda, New Georgia, and from which their aircraft were harrying the South Solomons, could be seized with a reasonable economy of force if this was done as soon as practicable and would prove an excellent forward air base for further Allied advances.

However before the attack on New Georgia could be mounted, the Russell Islands, thirty five miles north west of Cape Esperance on Guadalcanal, had to be seized.

These islands are extremely fertile and have been found especially suitable for the growing of coconuts on the flat areas which comprise the greater part of the little group. Consequently they have very little jungle and forest and the highest point is some way short of a mountain yet more than a hill. On Pavuvu island in 1942 two Lieutenants, Andresen and the author, had been landed by night to establish a Coastwatching station for the specific purpose of reporting on the Japanese barge traffic which was using the Russells as a ferrying base en route to Guadalcanal. After twelve days and several setbacks, not the least of which was a damaged transmitter, they had been on the point of establishing the station of Pavuvu Island when the sweep of events had rendered their presence there superfluous and they had been withdrawn to Guadalcanal. They had been able to bring with them an American airman who had been shot down and had been cared for by the local people, and were able to report that there were no Japanese in occupation and that the barge traffic had dwindled to almost nothing. Their reports had been transmitted to Divisional Intelligence but in 1943, when the invasion of the Central Solomons was under contemplation, this had apparently been forgotten and Lieutenant-Commander Mackenzie was asked to investigate the situation. He sent Lieutenants Andresen and Campbell over by night with a party of scouts and they reported that there were no Japanese on the Russells and no signs of recent traffic. This information was passed at once to the Divisional Intelligence staffs of General Vandergrift and Admiral Turner and also to Lieutenant-General M F Harmon, commander of all army troops in the South Pacific.

Despite this an operation known as CLEANSLATE was mounted using the bulk of the 43rd Infantry Division under command of Major-General J H Hester, the 3rd Marine Raider Battalion under command of Lieutenant-Colonel H B Liversedge, the 10th Defence Battalion Fleet Marine Force under Colonel R E Blake and other reinforcing Marine and army units. The intention was to invade the Russells, sweep the Japanese from them and establish a forward base and airfield. It would appear that the invading troops had not been told that the islands were empty of Japanese since on 21st February 1943 the 43rd Division stormed ashore on Banika Island intent on wiping out the Japanese only to be met by Lieutenants Andresen and Campbell with the offer of a cup of tea. The Marines, who knew a thing or two, landed at the same time on Pavuvu island without unduly exerting themselves.

The construction of an airstrip, a patrol torpedo boat base and a radar station was begun immediately and within four days the patrol boats were operating from Wernham Cove but it was not until the 6th of March that the Japanese reacted and delivered their first air attack, thereafter raiding the Russells constantly for the next four months. Despite the air attacks Allied aircraft began operating from the two strips laid out on Banika island on 15th April, and the Russells very soon became a major Allied forward operating base and staging area.

Operation Toenails

Admiral Halsey wanted information about the Japanese positions to be as precise and detailed as possible but this could not be done by air and naval attacks on the enemy positions which had little effect from the point of view of damage and provided no information of any value. The solution was to send a series of reconnaissance patrols into the New Georgia area to find out precisely what the situation was. The original plan of attack prepared by General de Witt Peck, the war plans officer of the South Pacific Command, had postulated an attack based on a division landing at Segi point on the south east tip of New Georgia where Major Kennedy had his Coastwatch headquarters, followed by a sweep westward to take Munda airstrip. Fortunately for all concerned General Harmon had serious doubts about the physical possibility of the plan from the time of its inception – indeed if anyone on the South Pacific Command staff had visited Segi they would have seen at once the impossi-

bility of the proposal. Segi had far too small a beach landing area and the invading troops would be faced with fifteen or more miles of very thick, trackless jungle and swamps before they reached the first Japanese outposts at Viru Harbour. There would then follow another similar stretch to Munda during which time they could expect to be ambushed, attacked continuously from the air and have the pleasure of the company of extremely wet, thick jungle and millions of mosquitos.

The first reconnaissance patrol was led by Lieutenant W Coultis, US Navy, accompanied by six Marines, and having contacted Major Kennedy at Segi they spent three weeks exploring the Roviana lagoon area, led at all times in and around the Japanese by his scouts. Never once during their tortuous and dangerous journeys were they in danger of being discovered so well were they led by Kennedy's

Marine raiders leave for the shore

scouts.

At the end of March, Lieutenant Coultis returned to Noumea and reported to Admiral Halsey that an assault on New Georgia was entirely practicable but not if based on the original plans. Meanwhile four other Marine amphibious patrols had been landed by Catalina at Segi and forwarded by Major Kennedy to the other Coastwatchers covering the Central Solomons area. The author, then a Lieutenant in the RANVR, provided scouts from his post on Rendova and his Marine party explored the Rendova shore-line and offshore islands. Lieutenant R Evans, RANVR, provided scouts for the Kolombangara area and the islands adjacent to it while Lieutenants H E Josselyn and R Firth, RANVR, did the same for the party exploring the area round Vella Lavella and Gizo. At all times the Marines were under the guidance and care of the local islanders and it says much for their good sense that they accepted the local people's advice and information and so kept out of trouble and garnered much useful information. These four patrols returned to Noumea by mid April and their information corroborated that supplied by Lieutenant Coultis.

Now the probing activities of the Marines and army amphibious patrols were intensified and the information which they brought back, combined with that provided by the Coastwatchers and aerial reconnaissance, made it clear that the Japanese had approximately 3,000 troops at Munda; 7,000 men on Kolombangara; about 500 on the Dragon peninsula and 300 in the Wickham anchorage area. On Rendova there were thirty- to forty-man units at Ughele village, Rendova plantation and Baniata point. Also there was an enemy unit at Lever Harbour on the north coast of New Georgia acting as an enemy coastwatching post, of about thirty men. It was also estimated that there were some 400 Japanese aircraft based on Rabaul which could be called up at short notice. Taking all this information into account Admiral Halsey's staff began to form their plan for the taking of Munda.

The plan envisaged first a seizure of Wickham Anchorage and Viru Harbour as staging points for small craft followed by seizure of the area round Segi point for the construction of an airstrip. The main landing would be on the shores of Rendova island and this area would form the springboard from which the attack on Munda could be launched. A Patrol Boat base would be constructed inside Rendova Harbour and attacks on Kolombangara and the north coast of New Georgia would also be staged from there.

Simultaneously Admiral Halsey's Third Fleet was to provide naval support and General MacArthur's forces would mount operations at Nassau Bay in New Guinea, in the Woodlark islands and in the Trobriands which would protect the southern flank of the Central Solomons. At the same time South West Pacific air forces were to attack Japanese airfields in the Bismarcks and Northern Solomons. As in most cases this plan was altered by circumstances and the final plan was in fact organised by Admiral Turner and his staff.

The reports of the amphibious scouting patrols had made it clear that landings and attacks could be made from points much closer to Munda than had previously been envisaged and Admiral Turner therefore divided his forces into two groups – Western Force and Eastern Force. Western Force, which he controlled personally, was to seize Rendova Island, Munda and Bairoko Harbour and adjacent positions while the Eastern Force commanded by Admiral G H Fort was to take Wickham Anchorage, Segi Point and Viru Harbour. The Western Force was again divided into several parts. General Hester was to command the landing force which consisted of the 43rd Infantry Division, the 3rd Battalion of the

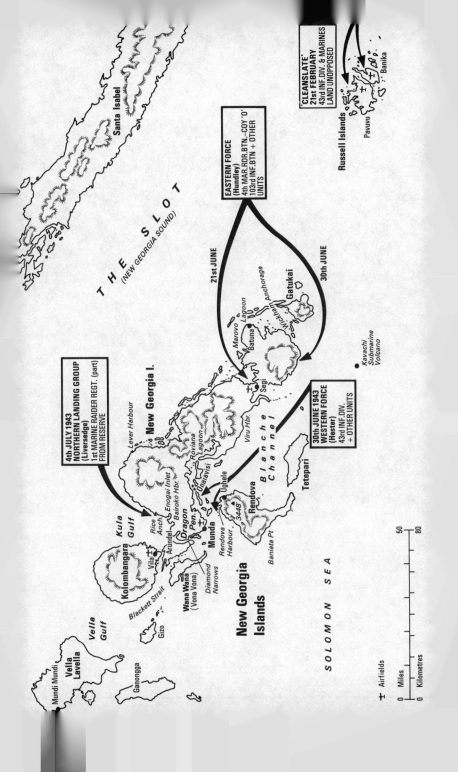

'CLEANSLATE'
21st FEBRUARY
43rd INF.DIV. & MARINES
LAND UNOPPOSED

Banika

Russell Islands

Pavuvu

EASTERN FORCE
(Hundley)
4th MAR.RDR.BTN.—COY 'O'
103rd INF.BTN + OTHER
UNITS

21st JUNE

30th JUNE

Marovo Lagoon

Batuna

Wickham Anchorage

Gatukai

Kavachi
Submarine
Volcano

Santa Isabel

T H E   S L O T
(NEW GEORGIA SOUND)

Segi

Viru Hbr.

Blanche Channel

Tetepari

30th JUNE 1943
WESTERN FORCE
(Hester)
43rd INF.DIV.
+ OTHER UNITS

4th JULY 1943
NORTHERN LANDING GROUP
(Liversedge)
1st MARINE RAIDER REGT. (part)
FROM RESERVE

Lever Harbour

New Georgia I.

Enogai Inlet

Bairoko Hbr.

Roviana Lagoon

Onaiavisi

Ughele

Baniata Pt.

Kula Gulf

Rice Anch.

Dragon Pen.

Arundel

Munda

3448

Rendova

Rendova Harbour.

Vila

Kolombangara

Wana Wana
(Vona Vona)

Diamond Narrows

Blackett Strait

Gizo

Ganongga

Vella Gulf

Vella Lavella

Mundi Mundi

New Georgia Islands

S O L O M O N   S E A

✝ Airfields

0   50
Miles
0   80
Kilometres

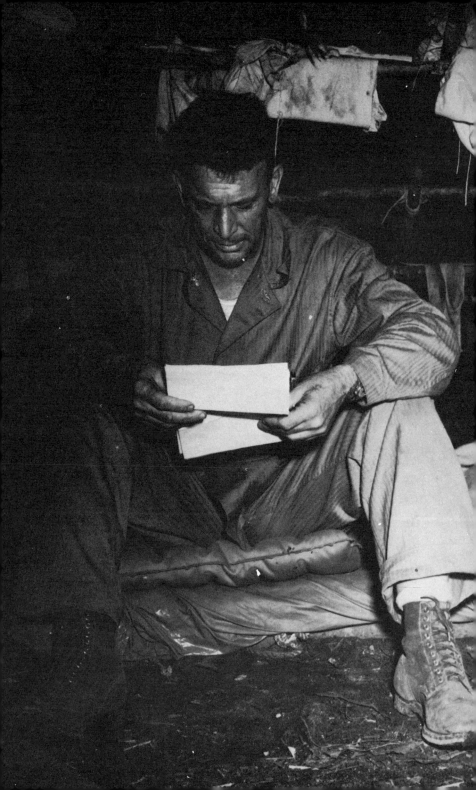

103rd Infantry, and the 136th Field Artillery Battalion the US Army; the greater part of the 20th and 24th Naval Construction Battalions; the 1st Company, the 1st Battalion, 1st Fiji Infantry; the 9th Marine Defence Battalion and Company O of the 4th Marine Raider Battalion of the Fleet Marine Force.

The Eastern Landing Force under Colonel D H Hundley, US Army, comprised the rest of 103rd Infantry Regiment; the 2nd Battalion 70th Coast Artillery; the 4th Raider Battalion under Lieutenant-Colonel C M Currin less Company O, and a number of specially assigned service units. The ready reserve consisted of the 1st Marine Raider Regiment less the 2nd, 3rd, and 4th Battalions and was commanded by Colonel H B Liversedge. In general reserve was the 37th Infantry Division Reinforced commanded by Major-General Beightler, US Army. Later the Naval Base Force under Captain C E Olsen, US Navy, and the New Georgia Air Force under General Mulcahy were to become part of the occupation force.

The intention was that Western Force would seize Rendova and its outlying islands while simultaneously Eastern Force occupied Viru Harbour, Segi Point and Wickham Anchorage by landings carried out after dark or at first light on 30th June 1943. Then on 1st, 2nd and 3rd July APDs (Assault Purpose Destroyers – i.e. converted First World War destroyers) and smaller craft would run in additional troops and supplies from the Russells and Guadalcanal by night thus avoiding Japanese air attacks. As soon as possible a fighter strip would be constructed at Segi point, through the plantation once owned by Markham, and from there fighter cover would be available to form an umbrella over the drive on Munda. At the same time Western Force would emplace 105mm howitzers and 155mm guns ('Long Toms') on the islands of Bau and Kokorana which guarded the entrance to Rendova harbour. These guns would bombard Munda Point and support the infantry. On the northern side of Blanche Channel, Sergeant

Left: **Colonel Harry B Liversedge reads a letter from home.** *Below:* **Vice-Admiral Halsey (left) with Brigadier-General De Witt Peck**

Harry Wickham of the British Solomon Islands Defence Force and a Coastwatcher, was to assemble his scouts with eighteen canoes and meet a 1st Marine Raider Battalion patrol led by Captain Clay Boyd. The combined unit would then mark out a boat channel from the Onaiavisi entrance of the Roviana lagoon to Zanana Beach near Bana Island about 1,400 yards north east of Egolo village on the south coast of New Georgia, as this was the only beach in the vicinity suitable for assault landings. The 1st Marine Raider Regiment was either to make a direct assault on the Enogai-Bairoko area or on the Roviana Lagoon beaches. If this latter course was adopted the force hoped to move overland through the jungle to Bairoko and there attack and destroy the enemy garrison. In either event Admiral Turner hoped to begin action by D Day plus four.

During this period Colonel Liversedge was to provide General Hester with six five-man Marine patrols whose duty it would be to reconnoitre vigorously the south coast of New Georgia in order to find suitable approach tracks from the beach area round Egolo towards Munda so that the forces under General Hester which should be ready in strength by 4th July, would cross from Rendova and making use of the tracks launch their attack on Munda. At the same time the Raider Regiment was to occupy the Bairoko-Enogai area to prevent movement of reinforcing Japanese

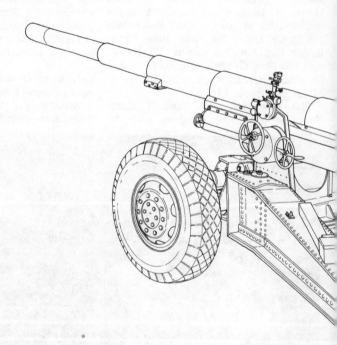

The US Model 1917A1 155mm gun (mounted on an M2 carriage). *Calibre:* 155mm. *Length overall:* 31 feet 10 inches. *Height:* 6 feet 2 inches. *Width:* 8 feet 10 inches. *Weight:* 25,905 pounds. *Muzzle velocity:* 2,410 feet per second. *Range:* 20,000 yards. *Rate of fire:* 4 rounds per minute. *Ammunition:* HE (95 lbs in weight), AP (100 lbs in weight), chemical and shrapnel. *Propellant charge:* 20-26 lbs

troops from Kolombangara to Munda. Finally, when Munda and Bairoko had fallen and the enemy on New Georgia had been destroyed, the Allied Force on New Georgia would attack Kolombangara.

Despite the simplicity and directness of the plan the fortunes of war saw it changed many times before it became an operational order. In the first place the Japanese began implementing a Japanese High Command decision taken early in May to hold the Central Solomons. This defence was entrusted to a joint command in which General Hitoshi Imamura commanding the Japanese Eighth Army, whose area covered the Bismarcks, New Guinea and the Solomons, was responsible for the dispositions of army troops and Admiral Jinichi Kusaka, commanding the Japanese Southeast Area Fleet was responsible for the disposition of the combined Special Landing Forces of Japanese

Marines and other personnel as well as naval coverage of the area. As a result the Japanese defenders, who numbered about 9,000 men in early May, were augmented before 30th June by some 2,400 men brought forward from Rabaul and Bougainville to Munda.

The Coastwatchers and aerial observation kept the Allied Intelligence staff aware of what was happening and this led Admiral Turner to ask for extra forces in the shape of two reinforced Infantry divisions, three Marine Defence Battalions, four Marine Raider or Parachute Battalions and 14,000 other troops. His request was unsuccessful but subsequent events proved that he had not underestimated the difficulties of the task. The majority of Allied forces were coming new to the battle and had yet to win their spurs and Admiral Turner knew from experience during the fight for Guadalcanal that to

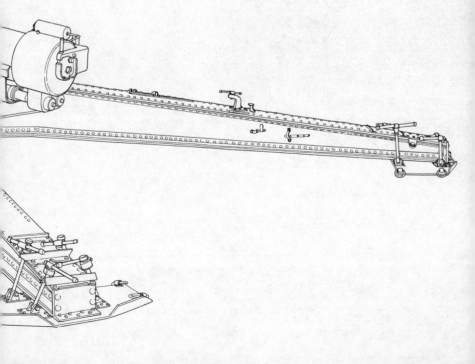

cope with the battle-trained, hard hitting Japanese fighting man the Allies would need an overwhelming superiority in men and materials if the struggle was not to be a long drawn out affair.

Meanwhile patrols continued their probing in the area and a week later Captain Clay Boyd returned from one such patrol to report that it would take about a month for the Raider Regiment to move from Zanana to Bairoko because of the very thick jungle, the extreme difficulty of the terrain and the enemy opposition which was sure to be encountered en route. Boyd also reported that the nature of the reefs and other obstructions in the Roviana lagoon would make it impossible to make rapid landings therein on the scale envisaged. Admiral Turner thereupon decided that the Marine Raider Regiment would land at Rice Anchorage on the western shore of New Georgia.

The Western landing force consisted of a large number of units and General Hester decided that to deal with their activities over a wide front his divisional staff would have to be split into two segments. One, under General Hester, would supervise the activities of the Occupation Force as a whole, while the other under Brigadier-General L F Wing, would be responsible solely for the first landing on Rendova Island. The plans followed the broad outlines laid down by Admiral Turner but inevitably were greatly modified by events, the first of which proved a blessing in disguise. It involved the seizure of Segi Point by half of the 4th Marine Raider Battalion on 21st June, followed the next day by additional units from General Hundley's force. This meant that the timetable had to be readjusted for the Eastern Landing Force and troops whose tasks had been allocated were switched to other commitments. However this 'premature' invasion of the New Georgia area had the favourable effect of permitting completion of the fighter strip ten days before schedule and came about owing to the activities of Major D G Kennedy, DSO, the Coastwatcher at Segi.

Left: **Vice-Admiral Jinichi Kusaka, C-in-C South East Area Fleet**
Below: **General John Hester**

Battle is joined

The saga of the Coastwatchers in the Solomons has been told elsewhere but for a proper understanding of the events in the New Georgia fighting it is essential to understand the background of their work in the Central Solomons which made the Allied invasion very much easier. In 1942 there was no force in the Solomons with which to meet the advancing Japanese. In times of peace the Armed Constabulary had been a small body of men armed with antiquated .303 rifles and quite inadequate to cover let alone defend the enormous area of the Solomons. The decision was taken to evacuate all civilians and those Government officers who were without posts owing to the advance of the enemy. All that remained of the administration was the Resident Commissioner and five District Officers together with several planters and missionaries who had elected to stay behind. Some of these men and the District Officers had been members of the Coastwatching service in peace time and their work had been Intensified at the outbreak of war. The Royal Australian Navy had an intelligence liaison officer in the shape of Lieutenant MacFarlan, RANVR, stationed on Guadalcanal and he was responsible for the coordination of all signals and Intelligence reports sent in from the Coastwatching network which also tied in with the civilian radio contacts maintained by the Resident Commissioner, for the District Officers continued to carry out the administration of their Districts. This had the effect of convincing the islanders that their faith in His Majesty's Government was justified and that they would be led by the people to whom they were accustomed and who they trusted in their fight against the Japanese. It also enabled the District Officers to take steps for the safety of the people and their villages and food supplies, for all the islanders

US Marine sniper takes aim

were warned of what to expect and arrangements were made for villages and gardens on the coast to be moved to the high bush which, it was hoped, would not be so vulnerable to attack from the enemy.

At the beginning of 1942 the District Officers were spread throughout the Solomons: Colin Wilson was on Vanikoro in the area of the Eastern Outer Islands: Michael Forster was in charge of San Cristobal and Ugi, Ulawa and the Three Sisters Islands: Martin Clemens was on Guadalcanal: Charles Bengough was in charge of Malaita; and it was to Malaita that the Resident Commissioner, William Sydney Marchant, transferred his headquarters from Tulagi when it became clear that the Japanese had invaded the islands. Donald Kennedy had charge of the Western and Central Solomons and also the District of Ysabel which included the Russell islands. Kennedy had the largest area to cover and he did this to great effect using his District vessel the *Wai-ai*. He had organised the Headmen in the Districts and villages so efficiently that they maintained their administrative duties throughout the war, quite apart from supplying a continuous flow of Intelligence about the enemy, and providing scouts, a very effective rescue service and transport and other assistance whenever called upon to do so. The loyalty of the islanders was unwavering and they gave their services and in some cases their lives without thought of reward. They formed guerilla bands and enrolled in the British Solomon Islands Defence Force when it was revived after the invasion of Guadalcanal by the United States Marines.

The Solomon islanders were particularly adept in their own particular form of ambush warfare, being so effective that in late 1942 and thereafter Japanese units would not venture into the bush unless in considerable strength as smaller patrols seldom returned. These disappearances had a tremendous effect on the morale of the Japanese and they did not help themselves by their exceptionally stupid behaviour towards the islanders and their possessions. Perhaps the most foolish thing they did was to destroy the native gardens they found. In the primitive conditions of the Solomons each family would make its own garden by the very laborious method of burning off the jungle, cutting down the large trees and then clearing the land and planting such crops as sweet potatoes, yams, taro etc by the use of pointed digging sticks so that, by careful husbandry, there was food for the whole family if only enough for each day was taken at any one time. But this meant nothing to the Japanese who would wantonly destroy a whole year's work in one visit to a garden. Nothing infuriated the islanders more, and when in addition the Japanese smashed their canoes and desecrated their churches it was small wonder that the islanders took their revenge whenever they could.

Kennedy had his first brush with the enemy when near the Shortland islands in early 1942. He was attacked in the *Wai-Ai* by a Japanese float plane which despite five strafing runs failed to hit the vessel. This did not deter Kennedy from continuing with his reconnaissance and later radioing in his report. (All Coastwatchers reported throughout the twenty-four hours on a secret wave length although there were always problems with 'skip distance' at night when it was usually impossible to get signals through.) He continued his tour of the Western District, fortunately he was not spotted again, and then returned to his headquarters on Ysabel and continued on to visit Rennell Islands south of Guadalcanal where he established an alternative base in case he was forced to move out of the Western and Central Solomons.

It was not long after this that the Japanese entered the Solomons in strength and invaded Tulagi and landed on Guadalcanal in 1942. This left Kennedy behind the enemy lines and much too close to the enemy for his safety or comfort. The Japanese soon began probing the areas round Tulagi and the islands of Gela and Ysabel and as a consequence of one of their raids in an armed barge his ship the *Wai-Ai* had to be sunk at her moorings to prevent her capture by the enemy. Kennedy and his men had a very narrow escape and he decided to move further north deeper into enemy territory. He had already made alternative arrangements for shipping and stores and decided to make his base at Segi passage at the south-east end of New Georgia. His reasoning was based on the fact that the Admiralty chart showed foul ground and he thought it unlikely that the Japanese would attempt to enter the passage. He had previously made sure that the passage had in fact a good deep water landing strip for flying boats and that shipping of fair tonnage could enter the passage if piloted with caution. The other advantages of Segi as a headquarters were that it was a natural focus for canoe routes from the Marovo lagoon and the Blanche Channel and from Tetepari Island. The few bush tracks also converged there and in addition there was good accommodation in Harold Markham's plantation house alongside the waters of the passage.

Since Kennedy was now deep inside enemy held territory he was cut off from supplies of food; he had very few offensive weapons and his stocks of ammunition were low. He therefore devised a strategy which at once enabled him to feed and arm his small force and at the same time to raise the morale of the people of New Georgia. Much of the Japanese traffic in men and material was carried in barges and it was these which became Kennedy's target. His scouts or the people from the villages would locate barge hideouts and if they were in striking distance from Segi, Kennedy and his men would ambush them at night, killing the crews and removing arms and food after which the barge would be sunk and the crew handed over to the

sharks. Often the Japanese were faced with mysterious disappearances of barges and crews. It was particularly important that no Japanese patrols or barges should be allowed near Segi passage lest they discovered the location of the Coastwatching station and the meagreness of Kennedy's resources, and Kennedy's policy was to attack and destroy all such intruders. In this he received notable help from his second in command, Bill Bennett, the son of a European father and an island mother. Bill was a very versatile young man having been at various times a medical dresser, primary school teacher, cook boy, maritime mechanic and deck hand. He proved himself expert in the peculiar kind of guerilla warfare in which Kennedy engaged.

In action he showed courage of the highest order. On one occasion Kennedy led a night attack on two armed barges full of troops which had moored alongside a mangrove covered shore. The barges were raked with machine gun fire and the detachment then crawled within range and threw grenades under the awnings until the counter fire from the barges appeared to have ceased. But it was quite possible that the Japanese were lying doggo and to make quite sure that they had been wiped out Bill Bennett went forward alone with his tommy gun, crawled under the awnings and emerged a few minutes later to announce that the crews were indeed dead. Kennedy's men then rapidly removed all ammunition and food from the barges, unshipped their machine guns, sank the barges after dropping the dead Japanese into the sea and, having removed all traces of the conflict, faded away into the jungle leaving one scout to report on any follow up. Two days later the scout returned to Segi and reported that a heavily armed Japanese patrol had made its way cautiously to the approximate area of the action and then returned to Munda clearly puzzled and showing obvious signs of unease in the dark and

The Consolidated PBY Catalina series of long-range maritime reconnaissance amphibians is probably the most successful flying-boat design ever produced. The type was built in Russia under licence, no numbers being available for aircraft produced there, but 3,290 Catalinas were built in the United States and in Canada, serving with the air forces of most of the Allies in the Second World War, and remaining in service with several of the world's smaller air forces to this day. Illustrated is a PB2B of the Royal Australian Air Force. The PB2B was distinguishable from the standard Catalina by its taller vertical tail surfaces, which was introduced

Martin Clemens, Coastwatcher, with some of his native constables

turned his ship towards it. At first the enemy rowed frantically in the other direction but when they saw that they could not escape, they turned about and made straight for the *Dundavata*.

Kennedy opened fire at 500 yards and got in three and a half drums from the Browning before it jammed. The Japanese had opened fire on the ketch at the same time and an unlucky bullet hit Kennedy in the thigh but he kept on firing. The enemy fire fell away and Kennedy gave the order 'Full speed ahead – ram the enemy'. The *Dundavata* raced along at a majestic seven knots and as she crashed into the whaleboat the guerillas threw a shower of grenades into the Japanese but there was no real need, for the whaleboat capsized under the impact of the *Dundavata* and as she turned about for another run they could see many corpses floating on the surface. But there was no time to lose. The bodies were brought ashore, stripped, searched and buried and the whale-boat having been divested of all gear and food was sunk in the lagoon while the guerillas dived for equipment which had been lost by the Japanese.

Back at Segi Kennedy was lucky to find Flight-Lieutenant Corrigan, RAFVR, one of the Coastwatchers who had been sent up on a fact finding mission and he was able to take over Kennedy's duties and look after him until his leg healed.

The demeanour of the prisoners taken by Kennedy had changed markedly since the early days of 1943. At first they had been arrogant and cheerful and had tried everything to induce him to release them even writing him a letter in impeccable English offering him 'the status of a first class prisoner' and 'every kindness and consideration' if he would free them and have them taken to Rabaul. By the time the author had arrived and the prisoners were removed to Guadalcanal in the Catalina which had brought him to Segi, the outlook of the Japanese captured up to that date had changed to one of gloom and despondency as they saw more and more Allied planes flying north and returning while of their own there was no sign. So the Allies had another advantage when finally the assault on New Georgia began, and that was a comparatively low morale amongst the Japanese forces who, by then, had probably realised that they could not win the war but were determined to fight on as long as they could.

The nearest Japanese unit to Segi was at Viru harbour to the north-west and consisted of 245 men of the 229th Infantry Regiment of the Imperial Japanese Army under the command of First Lieutenant Takagi, and some naval personnel. It was not long after the Battle for Marovo Lagoon that General Sasaki decided to attack Segi and for this task he decided to use Major Hara's 1st Battalion which was the parent unit of the 3rd Company at Viru Harbour. Accordingly Major Hara moved to Viru and began a programme of intense patrol activity aimed at 'smoking out' Kennedy and his men. Strong enemy patrols probed down the coast, and the villages and trails between Viru harbour and Segi point were investigated. Kennedy's scouts reported the presence of the Japanese and Kennedy realised that he would not be able to hold Segi for long. He knew, too, the vital importance of Segi to the Allied plan of attack and he thereupon sent a Most Urgent signal through Lieutenant-Commander Mackenzie to Admiral Turner requesting reinforcements without delay.

The request was received at Turner's headquarters during the night of the 18th June, and Turner acted immediately. The 4th Marine Raider Battalion (less Companies N and Q who were scheduled to attack Vangunu Island) plus A and D Companies, 103rd Infantry US Army, were embarked on the destroyer transports *Dent*, *Waters*, *Schley* and *Crosby* on the evening of 20th June, and sailed at high speed for Segi where they were guided in by

USS Dent (APD-9) 4th Marine Raider Battalion transport

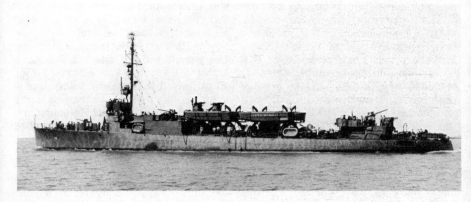

USS Schley, also a transport of 4th Marine Raider Battalion

USS Crosby which, with *Dent*, *Waters* and *Schley* brings troops to Segi

Kennedy's men and landed their Marines by assault at 0530 next morning. They were followed by the two army companies on the succeeding day and the next week saw the Marines and the army units systematically combing the area round Segi without contacting the enemy although there was ample evidence that they had been there. Meanwhile the programme for Segi was put forward and the Seabees (naval construction units) whose job it was to build the fighter strip at Segi, began work. They pushed ahead with such effect that on the ninth day after the landing at Segi an American plane, damaged over Munda, landed on the strip and by the twelfth day the Segi fighter airfield had saved sufficient aircraft damaged or out of fuel to pay for its own cost. Kennedy's main role now was one of liaison with the many and diverse forces coming ashore and this entailed the provision of guides, the passing of messages over his teleradio and general assistance of all kinds. He abandoned his Segi headquarters and moved across the passage to enable his administration and his scouts and guerillas to be kept separate from the many skirmishes and ambushes building up on the mainland of New Georgia.

The putting forward of the Segi operation had somewhat disrupted Admiral Turner's original plans but a very valuable foothold had been gained in the New Georgia area without loss to the Allies which enabled an earlier build up of troops and supplies and aircraft than had been anticipated. This made things easier for the advance overland to Viru Harbour but it soon became clear to Colonel Currin, in command of the 4th Raider Battalion, that Admiral Fort's original order was based on incorrect assumptions about both the terrain between Segi and Viru Harbour and the enemy resistance likely to be encountered

AA post, part of defence preparations at Segi Point

since the increase in Japanese forces at Viru Harbour after the arrival of Major Hara and his men. Viru Harbour lay eleven air miles from Segi but to reach it by land small and tortuous trails which had to pass round the headwaters of unfordable streams increased the actual distance to be travelled. Furthermore the original reconnaissance had been by small, lightly armed patrols which could move much more quickly than the large combat units equipped for assault, and these had given wrong impressions of the time taken to move men and equipment between the two places.

Colonel Currin therefore signalled Admiral Fort for permission to land at Regi village a mile east of Nono village (which was held by an undetermined number of Japanese), to use Company O as well as Company P and to begin operations on 27th instead of 28th June. His request was granted and on the night of 27th June the Marines embarked from Segi in their rubber boats and paddled along the coast to Regi, landing there at 0015 next morning. As dawn broke they set off along the narrow trail towards Viru with Company O leading followed by the Headquarters Company and with Company P as rearguard. Some three hours later a Japanese patrol bumped into the end of the column and in the ensuing fire fight, four of the five-man Japanese patrol were killed. At 1115 another enemy group attacked the rearguard and this developed into an hour-long skirmish in which heavy machine guns were brought to bear on the enemy until they broke off the action and withdrew.

The delays brought about by these encounters together with the very difficult terrain of steep hills, flooded streams, heavy jungle and coral outcrops slowed down the advance to such an extent that Colonel Currin realised that he could not reach Viru harbour on schedule and sent a message to Admiral Turner saying that he would be a day late. The next day the advance continued without incident until at 1400, as Company P crossed the Choi river, Captain Walker despatched Lieutenant Brown with sixty men to investigate a commanding piece of high ground to the right of the trail. It was as well that he did so for the enemy were dug in on the crest of the hill and a fight developed. Currin heard the sound of the firing and as he could not raise Walker on the radio and no runner appeared he returned as fast as possible to Walker's position arriving just as the enemy broke off the action and fled carrying their wounded but leaving eighteen dead while Lieutenant Brown's unit had five men killed and one wounded. This further delay resulted in a bivouac for the night at the headwaters of the Choi and on 30th June, the Marines were still a day's march from Viru harbour.

That morning the Viru occupation unit consisting of Captain R E Kinch and his landing force, carried aboard the USS Hopkins, Kilty and Crosby, were standing off Viru Harbour but were quite unable to raise Colonel Currin by radio. Eventually the ships began to move slowly shorewards and were fired on by a Japanese 3-inch gun on Tetemara Point, although according to the plan it should have been knocked out by the Marines. The ships withdrew out of range and Captain Leith, who was in command, obtained Turner's approval to put Kinch and his force ashore at Nono so that they could advance overland and assist the Marines if need arose. Meanwhile, as it transpired later, Major Hara reported to General Sasaki at Munda Point that the Viru Sector Unit had repulsed an American landing.

The Marines continued to advance towards Viru and on the night of the 30th found themselves within striking distance of the harbour with information from the Coastwatchers that the

Much needed supplies are landed for weary troops in the Viru harbour area

main strength of the enemy was concentrated near Tetemara village on the west shore of the harbour, and that there was a small outpost at Tombe village directly across the harbour from Tetemara. On the basis of this information two platoons of P Company were ordered to move against Tombe and to attack and destroy the enemy post there on 1st July. This attack was to be co-ordinated with an attack on the main Japanese force at Tetemara carried out by the remainder of Colonel Currin's unit.

The two platoons from P Company were in position by 0845. After a heavy burst of fire the Marines charged and cleared the village finding thirteen dead Japanese and suffering no casualties themselves. However the attack on Tetemara took far longer to complete although the troops were helped by six dive bombers which bombed and strafed the area, driving the enemy from the beach into the jungle. While the air attacks were in progress, the LCTs (Landing Craft, Tanks), loaded with fuel and ammunition for the proposed Patrol Boat base, moved into the harbour and stood by until the Marines had cleared the enemy from the landing area and it was safe to unload their supplies. At first the Marines met with slight opposition but as they advanced it became stiffer. At 1305 the Marines had reached high ground south-west of Tetemara where they dug in while demolition squads destroyed enemy machine gun posts. Then, at 1500 the attack was resumed and a final bayonet charge carried the position and the few remaining Japanese faded into the jungle. At 1700 the LCTs beached, dropped their ramps and began to discharge their cargo.

In the action forty-eight Japanese had been killed while the Marines had lost eight killed and fifteen wounded. They had also captured sixteen machine guns, one 3-inch gun, four 80mm guns and eight dual purpose guns together with much assorted ammunition, plus food, clothing, small boat stores and various miscellaneous items. The Marines immediately organised defence positions and three days later were joined by Company B, 103rd Infantry which had completed its march from Nono.

On 9th July a garrison force relieved the original units and the Marine Raiders returned to Guadalcanal to await further orders. They had lost thirteen killed and fifteen wounded in the two small actions at Tombe and Tetemara.

General Sasaki now ordered Colonel Hirata to abandon eastern New Georgia and bring back the remaining garrisons to help in the defence of Munda. In the end about 170 of Major Hara's original force reached Munda about 18th July in time to take part in the final defence of the airfield.

Vangunu Island, which is of volcanic origin, is separated from the south east tip of New Georgia by the narrow Njai Passage and beyond it to the south east Wickham Anchorage separates it from the smaller island of Gatukai. Lying some five miles south south east off Gatukai is the intermittently active submarine volcano whose local name is Kavachi. Earlier reports from Kennedy and more recent probings by amphibious Marine patrols had made it clear that only a small enemy unit was on Vangunu and its capture should not require the effort and expenditure of a large scale attack. Moreover it could not be bypassed as it would leave open to further enemy occupation an island having good sheltered harbours, although there were no areas on it suitable for an airstrip, and the harbours would help the Allied supply route between the Rendova-Munda target areas and the bases in the southern Solomons and for these reasons Admiral Turner decided that the island must be seized.

In mid June Lieutenant Schrier, who had been to the island during an earlier patrol, was sent back to make a last minute assessment of the situation. On 20th June he reported that there were few Japanese on Vangunu and that the beaches in the vicinity of Oloana bay would be able to take a reinforced battalion. Turner thereupon directed Admiral Fort to occupy the island and in turn Fort ordered Lieutenant-Colonel Brown of the US Army to carry out the mission using the 2nd Battalion, 103rd Infantry, Battery B, 7th Coastal Artillery, Companies N and Q and the Demolitions Platoon and the Headquarters Detachment of the 4th Marine Raider Battalion under Major R J Clark. The immediate objective was Oloana Bay in Wickham Anchorage where Turner wished to construct a staging point. The plan of attack was straightforward: the Marine group was to land before dawn from the APDs *Schley* and *McKean*, contact the reconnaissance party under Lieutenant Schrier who would have with him a group of Kennedy's scouts, and then establish a beachhead. The army battalion was divided into two groups. One would land thirty minutes

after the Marines and the other at 1000. The first group would occupy Vura village and the west bank of the Vura river in order to prevent the escape of the Japanese reported to be in the village. Meanwhile the remainder of the group would drive well inland and set up a force beachhead line behind which guns would be emplaced while the Seabees began the construction of a small naval base.

At 0335 on 30th June the *Schley* and *McKean* with the Marines aboard hove to off Oloana Bay in Wickham Anchorage but then the weather took a hand. Pitch darkness and heavy rain obscured the markers and signal lights put out by Schrier, and Admiral Fort decided to postpone the landing until dawn. But either his orders never reached the *Schley* and *McKean* or else they were ignored, for the APDs commenced unloading the

Heavy mortar fire is effective against Japanese positions, knocking out weapons and discouraging attacks

Marines as previously arranged and while doing so their commanders discovered that they were a thousand yards out of position and moved to the east accordingly, but as the landing craft manoeuvred into position for their run to the shore they inadvertently became tangled up with the LCTs carrying the army units. Their coxswains lost the tenuous contacts they had had and proceeded shorewards individually or in pairs landing at widely separated points. The sea had by now become very rough and six landing craft were wrecked on shoals or on reefs and this resulted in the widespread dispersal of units which should have landed as a compact whole.

At daylight, however, the first wave of infantry landed in good order and when Colonel Brown came ashore Lieutenant Schrier told him that the main body of the enemy had been located in Kaeruka village some thousand yards north east of Vura village. The Colonel promptly altered his plans, making Kaeruka the main objective. Oloana was to be defended by the Seabees and artillerymen while the rest of the assault force plus the Marines who had landed out of position, would use the trails cut by the scouts attached to Kennedy, which lay about seven miles to the north east along high ground running west to east behind the Kaeruka river and village, to get behind the Japanese force at Kaeruka. Finally after great exertions, the four companies were in position for the assault. Company Q was on the extreme right flank covering the east bank of the Kaeruka river. Company N in position next to Q would drive straight ahead for the enemy bivouac at the river mouth. Company F on their left would swing south west and envelop any resistance met in their area while Company G was held in reserve to exploit enemy weakness or to protect the flanks of the army and Marines.

The attack was launched at 1405 and took the Japanese completely by surprise. Their resistance stiffened and the ensuing fire fight ended when the Japanese positions were wiped out and the beach made secure by 1730. Company E, which had been left at Vura, was attacked at about the same time by sixteen of the enemy using two light machine guns but Captain Chappell using his mortars with skill knocked out the enemy weapons and the remainder of the Japanese scattered into the bush. Night was approaching as the action at Kaeruka finished and Captain Clark set up a defence perimeter as soon as possible. Meanwhile Colonel Brown had moved his command post from the departure point down to the defence perimeter on the beach while Clark sent out small patrols to kill or capture the few surviving enemy riflemen and to reduce the last hostile bunkers such as that which had caused trouble to Company Q. By the time the patrols had returned and despite the exhaustion of the men, the defence perimeter was well organised. During the night there was spasmodic firing from both sides and shortly before 0200 the following morning barges were heard approaching. Soon three Japanese barges headed into land between the junction of the Demolitions Platoon and Company G.

Heavy fire was directed on the barges, whose crews, thinking that the Japanese on shore had mistaken them for the Allies, shouted back not to fire and the barges continued towards the shore. By 0235 the fight was over. One barge sank in deep water some seventy yards offshore while the other two broached in the surf and 109 of the 120 Japanese were killed. The eleven survivors who managed to get ashore were killed on the beach some days later. Two marines and one soldier killed during the fight were buried with other American dead on the east bank of the Kaeruka after daylight. Documents had been taken from the enemy and these, when translated, showed that the barges were on a routine supply

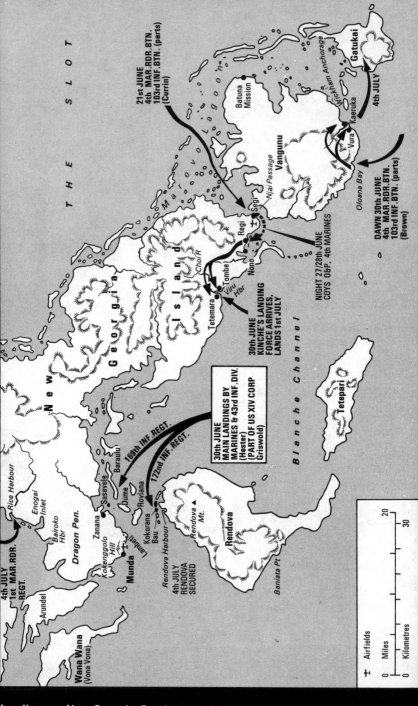

Landings on New Georgia, Rendova and Vangunu

Many streams have to be crossed in the advance. Fords are favourite ambush points for Japanese snipers

Troops clamber down nets to landing craft from Turner's flagship *USS McCawley*

run to the Japanese unit at Kaeruka and in fact the fresh provisions on the barges, which included chickens, soon became total casualties.

Next day patrols reported no contacts and Colonel Brown moved his entire force to Vura village which would provide a better base for operations and supply. While doing so the enemy opened up with machine guns and one 37mm gun which inflicted several casualties on the Marines but no organised attack followed and from Vura Colonel Brown conducted a campaign of attrition against the enemy using the 152nd Field Artillery and by this means and the use of numerous air strikes the remaining Japanese were either killed or captured. On 3rd July Brown led his forces back to Kaeruka killing seven of the enemy on the way and destroying Japanese ammunition and supply dumps which had been overlooked earlier.

During the night of 4th July Captain Clark took his men over to Gatukai island where scouts had reported between fifty and one hundred of the enemy and for the next two days the Marines searched the island but found no trace of the enemy although there were numerous traces of their earlier occupation. After this they returned to Oloana Bay and embarked on LCT 331 which landed them on Guadalcanal at 0700 on 12th July where they rejoined their parent battalion. The army units continued patrolling and mopping up but now Wickham Anchorage was secure. The action had cost the Marine Raider Battalion fourteen dead and twenty-six wounded.

The actions at Segi, Viru Harbour and Vangunu, although small in themselves, represented in miniature what was to be expected when the major battles in the New Georgia campaign took place. But whether or not there was time to convey the gist of the lessons learned (as to timing, difficulties of communication, the necessity of resting men who – because of lack of training were easily fatigued, the very difficult terrain and the incessant attacks of mosquitos, the onset of fever and the high temperature and humidity) to General Harmon and Admiral Turner is not known. Suffice to say the same lessons had to be learnt all over again in the months that followed.

While the Marines and army had been operating around Segi, at Viru Harbour and on Vangunu and Gatukai islands, preparations and rehearsals for the major invasion of the New Georgia mainland at Munda had been under way far to the south. The plan was to land the majority of the forces involved (US XIV Corps in part) on Rendova island, ferry them across to the New Georgia coast east of Munda and begin a co-ordinated drive along the south coast to take Munda airfield. The main operation would be carried out by the US Army but the Marines participation, although smaller, was vital to the success of the operation as indeed was the assistance rendered by the Coastwatching service and the units from Fiji, Tonga and the Solomon islands.

After the 172nd Infantry and the 24th Naval Construction Battalion carried out ten days training in the Espiritu Santo and Efate areas of the New Hebrides, Admiral Turner and General Hester decided that it would be possible to discharge all the troops and gear involved within five hours of the actual landing on Rendova. The task force was ready and loaded off Koli Point, Guadalcanal by 29th June, and the task force flagship (AP *McCawley*) wearing Turner's flag sailed at 1600 that afternoon. The weather was lowering with much mist and cloud but the convoy was seen by the Japanese submarine *RO*-103 as it cruised south of Gatukai and its Commander alerted the Japanese garrisons at Rabaul and Munda. As a diversion to the attack on New Georgia Task Group 36.1, under Rear Admiral W L Ainsworth, bombarded Kolombangara and the Shortland Islands and laid mines in Shortland's harbour at the same time as the convoy weighed anchor and proceeded towards the Blanche Channel, between Munda and New Georgia, but these moves, intended to disrupt the Japanese operations in the area, had little effect.

The Japanese had estimated correctly that an American offensive in the New Georgia area was imminent. Their submarine commanders, their reconnaissance aircraft and their outposts had reported unusual activity in and around the south Solomons and the New Georgia area and when the volume of radio traffic reached its peak about 15th June, General Imamura and Admiral Kusaka naturally assumed that the attack was about to take place. To make ready for the battle the air strength at Rabaul had been increased by the influx of experienced squadrons from Japan and Truk and a proportion of these had been sent forward to the bases at Buin and at Ballalae in the Shortlands. However, after 25th June the Allied radio traffic fell off perceptibly (since the Allied plans had been rehearsed and all was ready for the start of the campaign there was little need for it) and this, together with the absence of shipping in the Guadalcanal area, led the Japanese to revise their estimates and to call off temporarily the deployment of their air strength. So, on 30th June, when Task Force 31 began the attack, the enemy did not have sufficient air strength in their forward areas for an effective counterattack.

A week before D Day the author, the Coastwatcher on Rendova, began to receive additions to his staff. First there came Flight Lieutenant R A Robinson, RAAF (another Coastwatcher), and with him Coder Payne, RAN and Sergeant Halveston, US Army; they were to assist the author prior to D Day and take over the station (call sign: PWD) the day before as he was to go down to the shore to guide in the invading troops and thereafter place himself at the disposal of the commanding general to assist in all possible ways with guerillas and his local knowledge. A day later several officers from the US Artillery and Infantry together with Lieutenant Redden, US Navy, arrived. They had all been landed by Catalina flying boat at Segi and brought by night past the Japanese positions first by Kennedy's scouts and then by those from Rendova. The scouts and the islanders prided themselves that they never lost a man and never failed to pick up anyone from the sea or in the bush if they were within their range. Invariably they managed to spirit away the Allied servicemen they rescued to the nearest Coastwatcher who would look after them until they could be returned to their units. This rescue system gave the Allies a tremendous boost as they could be virtually certain of being found and looked after if they had to bale out or crashed in enemy territory, and it is small wonder that the Japanese issued orders to their men to shoot islanders on sight.

The scouts on Rendova were kept busy guiding the US Army officers inspecting areas on Rendova plantation which it was intended should be allocated to the various units who would land there on D Day. The artillery officers were particularly anxious to find sites for their 155mm and other guns. Unfortunately there were sizeable Japanese patrols moving about the area in which the landing was to take place and this made it very difficult for the scouts to show the officers the exact positions they wished to use. There were several narrow escapes from detection and the scouts very wisely shepherded the officers back to the author at the same time closing the tracks they had used by planting on them growing shrubs and vines. After they had carried out their reconnaissance the army officers were returned to their

Rear-Admiral Ainsworth

units by the 'underground' to report their findings but Lieutenant Redden remained on Rendova with the author and the other Coastwatchers. On the day before D Day Lieutenant Redden accompanied the author over the mountain and down to the shore of the west coast of the island together with four of their scouts. They remained hidden until dusk then embarked in a canoe and, slipping past the barge anchorages used by the Japanese, they paddled silently out to the islands of Bau and Kokorana which flank the entrance to Rendova harbour. They made sure the islands were free of Japanese and then on Bau island Lieutenant Redden fixed a light facing seawards. This was to be flashed at 0500 to guide in a raiding party known as the Barracudas whose task it was to attack and destroy the Japanese outpost in Rendova plantation so that the army troops landing

USS Zane which grounded on an uncharted reef near Rendova harbour

later would be unopposed.

At 0500 Lieutenant Redden turned on the light and it shone strongly seaward for the prescribed three minutes. The night was extremely dark and from the islands the anxious watchers could see no answering flashes nor could they hear the rumble of engines or see the silhouettes of the invasion fleet. There was nothing for it but to spend the rest of the night in bivouac on Bau island.

As Admiral Turner's task force approached Rendova along the Blanche Channel during the very early hours of D Day (30th June) heavy fog came down and rain blotted out the landmarks. Nevertheless at 0230 APDs *Dent* and *Waters* hove to and the Barracuda unit led by their guide, Lieutenant F A Rhoades, RANVR, a Coastwatcher, scrambled over the sides into the waiting landing craft. The wind and the current proved contrary and the landing craft were carried miles from their objective and in fact did not reach it until ten

minutes after the first wave of army troops had been landed in Rendova harbour in the belief that the way was clear for them. The coxswains of the Army landing craft, thinking that the beaches were clear, vied with each other to get their troops ashore first. This happy state of affairs soon ceased and all became confusion tinged with not a little dismay as the first troops were met with machine gun fire from the Japanese. It was realised, somewhat belatedly, that the Barracudas had not cleared the beachhead and that the incoming troops would have to fight for it. For most of them it was their baptism of fire and as more and more craft came in and more and more troops and equipment piled up on the beach the situation became chaotic.

The already bad situation was not improved by a mounting hysteria as coxswains on incoming landing craft sprayed the beaches and coconuts indiscriminately with machine gun fire which only ceased when an officer on the beach threatened to shoot back. Meanwhile the infantry groped their way forward for some thirty yards until some marksman killed a sniper in a tree some seventy five yards inland. There followed a rush for souvenirs which advanced the skirmish line willy nilly but it was not until Colonel Ross, the commander of the 172nd, appeared on the scene that order was restored. He sent out combat patrols of soldiers and marines and chased the small Japanese force back into the hills and jungle at the foot of the mountain. Thereafter the build up continued and supplies poured ashore much faster than they could be handled and Rendova plantation became a quagmire and a scene of utter confusion. Nor did the weather help. Continuous heavy rain bogged down everything except the very wide tracked prime movers used for hauling the 155mm guns and these had to be pressed into service to pull every kind of equipment. Shortly after the troops had reached the shore a single Jap-

491

Above: USS Farenholt to which Turner transferred his flag. *Below:* 'Green Dragons' aboard LSTs move through a channel at Rendova harbour

anese twin engined bomber, apparently on reconnaissance, sighted the Task Force which immediately went to action stations while the bomber was driven off by the fighter patrol overhead.

The author and his scouts had come ashore and were kept busy providing information of all kinds and in order to keep clear of the chaotic conditions ashore the Coastwatchers set up temporary headquarters on a small island just off shore in Rendova harbour. It was there next morning that he was contacted by a very tired scout from the Coastwatchers hideout on the mountain. Apparently the Japanese who had been chased off the beach had retreated up the mountain and had stumbled on the Coastwatchers. There followed a running fight during which the vital parts of the radio equipment and the codes had been rescued and the Coastwatchers had had to take to the jungle when the Japanese brought a light machine gun to bear on them. The author arranged for his men to have food and rest but he was on tenterhooks as to what had happened to the teleradio at his old headquarters. He was in urgent demand on shore and could not go back up the mountain immediately but fortunately Lieutenant Redden volunteered to take an Army squad back to the lookout on the mountain in order to secure it and next day the author was able to make his way back to the site of his old station where he found the Army in possession. The teleradio had been smashed but most fortunately, however, the Japanese had overlooked his store which had been built under an overhang of rock on the hillside below the Coastwatching station, and there he found his second teleradio intact. The next morning the Army unit and the author went back down the mountain and that afternoon the Coastwatching station under its old call sign of PWD was on the air again and passing not only its own traffic but also that of the Command Head-

quarters when their own circuits became jammed or for some other reason could not get through to base on Guadalcanal.

While the landing on Rendova was proceeding, Companies A and B of the 169th Infantry and the combined Commando unit of Fijians, Tongans and Solomon Islanders numbering 130 men disembarked from the destroyer transport *Talbot* and the destroyer minesweeper *Zane*, to seize the key islets of Sasavele, Dume and Baraulu. Here all went according to plan and the invading force contacted Captain Clay Boyd, US Marines, and Sergeant Frank Wickham of the Coastwatchers, and were led to their target areas without mishap. There was a brief fight which cleared a small number of enemy from the area opposite the three islets, but the only casualty was the destroyer *Zane* which grounded on an uncharted reef and remained exposed to enemy air attack until pulled clear by the tug *Rail* later in the day.

The Japanese force on Rendova consisted of approximately 200 men of the 2nd Company Kure 6th SNLF (Special Naval Landing Force) and detachments of the 7th Company 229th Infantry. Those who were not killed during the establishment of the beachhead escaped into the jungle and that night made their way either to another Japanese outpost at Baniata Point on Rendova (this was the group which attacked the Coastwatchers on Rendova mountain) or escaped to the New Georgia mainland where they joined in the defence of Munda airfield. Major General Sasaki at Munda was ready for the approach of Task Force 31 and believed that the Americans would land either at Lambeti plantation or Munda Point and therefore did not react strongly when the Americans landed on Rendova, believing it to be a diversionary move, and by the time he had realised what was happening it was too late for him to retaliate in strength.

Admiral Kusaka, in Rabaul, now

155mm 'Long Toms' arrive at Rendova
to pound Munda

took charge of the overall Japanese action against the Allied forces in and around New Georgia. He made use of the aircraft he had at Rabaul and in the Shortlands to launch an attack on the Rendova beachhead and the ships in the area just before noon on D Day. Thirty Zero fighters came in from the west to strafe the beachhead and they in turn were attacked by the Corsairs, Grummans and other Allied fighters flying a protective cover over the shipping and beachhead. Shortly after the attack had begun Zeros began to be shot out of the sky and the few remaining Japanese aircraft broke off the battle and fled northwards. At 1515 the enemy sent in another attack – this time the aircraft were mixed and a flight of torpedo bombers managed to secure a hit on the *McCawley* which caused Admiral Turner to transfer his flag

Higgins boats beached and shrapnel-scarred on a Rendova beach after a Japanese air strike

to the *USS Farenholt*. Later the *McCawley* was sunk in error by a US Patrol Torpedo Boat which, in the dark, mistook her for an enemy ship. The second Japanese air attack was again beaten off and the US Fighter Command claimed thirty enemy aircraft for the loss of four of their own.

A third attack came late in the afternoon when the Japanese used dive bombers supported by fighters but again the enemy were driven off with heavy losses while the build up of men and material on Rendova continued. Rear Admiral Merrill's 12th Cruiser Division had plastered the Buin-Shortland area for fifteen minutes earlier in the day hoping to neutralise the enemy airfields and these bombardments were to have been followed by strikes by Flying Fortresses of General McArthur's command on Rabaul aerodrome, together with Kahili, Munda and Vila airfields on the island of Kolombangara which were to be hit by aircraft from the COMAIRSOLS Strike Command. How-

ever, as was so often the case, the weather closed in preventing flying and the Japanese were able to operate from their south Bougainville airfields and launch the attacks described above.

The second day on Rendova was spent in consolidating the defences and trying to impose some sort of order on the chaos caused by the tremendous build up of materials and men on the inadequate beachhead. Battery A of the 9th Defence Battalion US Marines managed to get their 155mm 'Long Toms', which arrived in LSTs, into position by 1800 and during the day patrols from 169th Field Artillery Battalion, protected by 43rd Division infantrymen and South Pacific Scouts, landed on Roviana Island and selected sites to be occupied by the main body of the artillery on 4th July. An attempt at an attack by Japanese aircraft at 1015 was beaten off by the patrolling fighters with the loss of nine planes, but five of their pilots were rescued and brought back to the American lines by the Coastwatchers.

The third day on Rendova began with a very heavy storm which not only made a worse quagmire of the ground but also grounded the air cover so that, when the weather cleared in the afternoon, there were no Allied fighters to counter an attack by twenty-four twin engined Japanese bombers covered by forty-four fighters. For once the enemy came in from the south protected from observation by the bulk of Rendova mountain and the inexperienced army troops thought they were American B25s; the Marines, wiser by experience, shouted at them to take cover but it was too late and the bombs had dropped. They were mostly anti personnel bombs and their flying fragments caused a great deal of damage hitting the 43rd Division Medical Clearing Point, starting fires in the fuel dump and damaging boats in the naval boat pool. Several guns were damaged, the radar knocked out and

the cordite and small arms on the Battery A position were set alight, and bullets were flying in all directions for some time. To add insult to injury one bomb – a dud – landed squarely between the trails of a 155mm gun putting it out of action until the battalion bomb disposal officer removed it.

On a tiny peninsula occupied by the 24th Construction Battalion a gelignite dump exploded causing more damage than the bombs themselves. The small area of the peninsula was inexcusably crowded with soldiers, sailors and marines and sixty-four were killed and eighty-nine wounded. In all, that day, the Allies suffered over 200 casualties. The author had established his coastwatching camp on a small islet in the harbour and as the bombers swept over he and his men threw themselves flat on the coral escaping the withering blast of fragments which cut across the island and shredded the trees. Three of the scouts were not so lucky. They were in a canoe crossing to the island when the bombs dropped and one bursting nearby on the water spattered them with fragments hitting one man on the chest. The others paddled him to the island where, the author recalls, they said to him: 'We're frightened Master!' And he replied, 'So am I – but if we don't get this brother of yours to hospital he will die!'

A temporary stretcher was made and the man was carried back to the canoe and then paddled over to the LST doing duty as a casualty clearing station. Several days later the injured scout returned much improved and clutching a blanket given to him by the Medical Corpsmen. The Coastwatchers had lost a considerable amount of equipment on the mountain and the island and the author went back to their base on Guadalcanal to collect replacements. In the meantime Flight-Lieutenant Robinson moved the Coastwatcher camp to the perimeter of the beachhead on Rendova and continued to give in-

The Mitsubishi A6M5 Reisen (codenamed ZEKE by the Allies) was a development of the earlier A6M3, designed to be better able to hold its own against the newer Allied fighters beginning to appear in the Pacific. To this end it retained the clipped wings of the earlier model, but had the tips rounded and heavier gauge wing plating, in an attempt to give the A6M5 the necessary diving speed to keep up with Allied machines. In addition, thrust augmentation was achieved by the use of individual

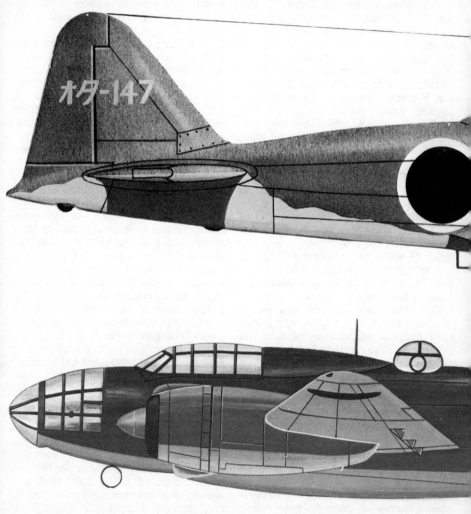

The Mitsubishi G4M3 land-based bomber (codenamed BETTY by the Allies) was the Imperial Japanese Navy's most famous bomber, and saw service in every theatre in which the navy was called upon to take a part, serving from beginning to end of the war. Because range was to be a vital component of the new bomber's success, the design team omitted all armour protection and self-sealing fuel tanks. This did indeed give the BETTY the range required for the early offensive stages of the war, but by the time the Allies were pushing forward in New Guinea and elsewhere, the BETTY was called upon to fly short-range defensive bombing missions against strong fighter opposition, where the lack of armour and self-sealing fuel tanks was

exhaust stacks. Despite these modifications, the A6M5 was still not a match for Allied types. *Engine:* one Nakajima NK1 Sakae 21 radial, 1,130hp at take-off. *Armament:* two Type 97 7.7mm machine guns and two Type 99 20mm cannon. *Speed:* 351mph at 19,685 feet. *Climb:* 7 minutes 1 second to 19,685 feet. *Ceiling:* 38,520 feet. *Range:* 1,194 miles maximum. *Weight empty/loaded:* 4,136/6,025 lbs. *Span:* 36 feet 1 $\frac{1}{16}$ inches. *Length:* 29 feet 11 $\frac{3}{32}$ inches

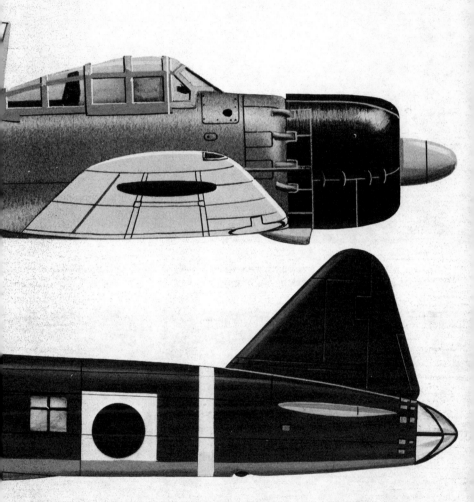

sorely felt, the type soon being dubbed 'The Flying Lighter'. In an effort to rectify these shortcomings, a better protected variant, the G4M3 Model 34, was produced, but this was too late to see any widespread service. *Engines:* two Mitsubishi MK4 Kasei radials, 1,800hp each at take-off. *Armament:* four Type 92 7.7mm machine guns and two Type 99 Model 1 20mm cannon as defensive armament, plus an offensive bomb load of 2,200 lbs or one 1,764 lb torpedo. *Crew:* seven. *Speed:* 272mph at 15,090 feet. *Climb:* 30 minutes 24 seconds to 26,245 feet. *Ceiling:* 29,365 feet. *Range:* 3,765 miles maximum. *Weight empty/loaded:* 17,990/27,558 lbs. *Span:* 82 feet 0 $\frac{1}{4}$ inches. *Length:* 65 feet 7 $\frac{13}{32}$ inches

Above: Anti-aircraft barrage beats off enemy planes. *Below:* Munda airfield
shows its wounds after attack by US bombers

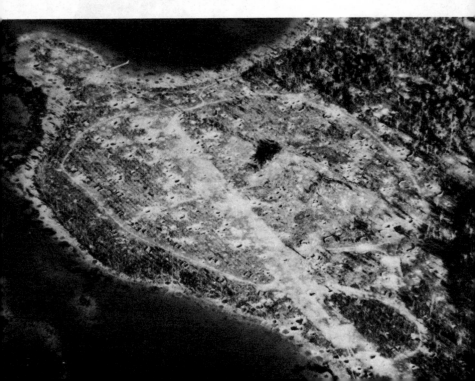

valuable assistance to the American forces. The air raid on the third day had revealed a number of defects in the planning and conduct of the operations. First: the Allies could not maintain a continuous fighter cover over Rendova from air fields on Guadalcanal and the Russells, especially if the weather was bad. Second: the air warning system failed because of dampness and the fact that at a rear supply base someone had put diesel fuel into a petrol drum and this had been used in the radar power unit with negative results. Third: the Coastwatchers could only report on information gathered in their areas and when they were prevented from doing so by the too close attentions of the enemy it left a blank in the Intelligence picture. Fourth: the troops were overcrowded and there had been no foxholes dug nor had shelters been constructed. Fifth: the army troops had not received sufficient training in aircraft identification and local anti-aircraft watches had not been kept.

At about 1730 the Japanese launched another air attack using two waves of twenty-five fighters but these were met by the re-established Allied air cover and broken up before they could reached the beachhead although six enemy planes and three Allied aircraft were shot down during the dog fights. That night (2nd-3rd July) General Hester began ferrying units of the 172nd Infantry across the Blanche Channel to New Georgia in order to build up his forces for the drive on Munda. Before dawn on 3rd July, the Japanese cruiser *Yubari* and nine destroyers attempted a bombardment of the Rendova beachhead and harbour but they were unable to hit the small beachhead and again bad weather hampered their sortie. All their shells fell harmlessly in the jungle and they retired harassed by Motor Torpedo Boats from Commander Kelly's squadron.

Truck convoy battles with mud to deliver rations to men in the field

Preparations continued during the 3rd of July for the movement of the greater part of the army and Marine forces across to the New Georgia mainland on 4th July. As a cover, artillery on Roviana island began to bombard the Munda and Lambeti plantation areas and the 155mm guns all registered on Munda airfield and Kokenggolo hill immediately behind it, and thereafter kept up intermittent shelling of the area. At 1400 there was an abortive attack by a mixed force of enemy fighters and bombers but they were driven off by an Allied air patrol which claimed to have destroyed six Japanese fighters and five bombers while admitting the loss of three of their own planes. At 1555 a counter-attack was made by forty-three torpedo bombers of strike command on Munda airfield. They were escorted by Marine, Navy, Army and New Zealand Royal Air Force pilots of fighter command and after completing their heavy attack without loss, they returned to their base on Guadalcanal. By the 4th July, Independence Day, Rendova could be considered to be reasonably secure although intermittent night raids continued.

In the event there was an attempt by the enemy to bomb both the Rendova and Zenana beachheads. At 1350 the radar picked up eighty planes approaching from the north-west. They came in over Munda and proved to be eighteen twin engined bombers at 8,000ft protected by sixty-six fighters at 14,800ft. The enemy fighters broke off to attack Allied fighter patrols over Munda, another flight south of Rendova and another flight just west of Rendova. All anti-aircraft guns were brought to bear – some without reason since they had not the range to reach out to the enemy aircraft – and the mixture of fighter aircraft and anti-aircraft barrage finally drove off the enemy but not before four bombers had dropped their loads killing six people and wounding thirteen, holing two

LCIs (Landing Craft Infantry) destroying a fuel dump and damaging some supplies. The actual number of enemy planes brought down was uncertain but since the enemy admitted to the loss of eleven, it was probably considerably more.

In the afternoon Strike Command again raided Munda with thirty-seven torpedo and dive bombers releasing twenty-eight tons of bombs and despite heavy anti-aircraft fire they returned without loss. General Hester was now forced by difficult terrain, the weather and enemy air attacks to alter the date of the full offensive by two days but the 9th Defence Battalion US Marines crossed to Zanana beach as scheduled just before dusk and, as night had fallen by the time had disembarked, it was not until morning that they were able to set up their .50 machine guns and 40mm guns.

The shore to shore movement from Rendova to New Georgia was resumed at daybreak on 5th July and, as on Rendova, it was not long before the tracks on New Georgia had been churned into a slimy morass so that supplies had to be manhandled from the shore to the dumps further inland. At 1230 the Coastwatchers on Vella Lavella sent an air raid alarm having spotted twin engined bombers on course for New Georgia. The Allied fighters were deployed over Rice Anchorage to protect the beachhead established there during the night of 4th July by the Marine Raider Regiment, and another force of fighters was on patrol over Wickham Anchorage, but there was no cover immediately over Rendova. As soon as the fighters received the Coastwatchers' report they moved to intercept the enemy who, however, did not approach Rendova but swung off to engage the army and New Zealand aircraft over Wickham Anchorage while the remainder of the flight tried to break through to the Russells. Fighter Command claimed destruction of six Zero fighters and ten

Officers survey a possible crossing

Above: USS Strong, sunk off Kolombangara by a Japanese long range torpedo
Below: Two Japanese survivors aboard a US vessel. Few allowed themselves
to be captured

ombers for the loss of two Allied ighters. That afternoon Munda was nce again attacked by an Allied force f twenty dive bombers and eighteen orpedo bombers armed with 1,000 nd 2,000-lb bombs. They were met by poradic anti-aircraft fire and suffer-ng no losses returned safely to ʈuadalcanal.

By dark the majority of the army orces on Rendova had been moved to he New Georgia beachhead but delays ontinued owing to the very difficult errain and the artillery kept up an ntermittent harassing fire on Munda etween the small beachheads and the nemy.

Admiral Kusaka had met the Allied ttack with uncoordinated responses n sea and in the air and consequently he areas he had attempted to defend ad fallen to the Allies without any erious delay to them. The Central olomons, with their very difficult errain and broken chain of islands llowing of penetration at innumer-ble points, needed a vast number of roops to defend them successfully; n fact the aggressor had most of the dvantages provided that he had ommand of the sea and air and this he Allies had now succeeded in chieving.

On 4th July, Admiral Kusaka and ʒeneral Imamura conferred at Rabaul nd bearing in mind the Imperial ʒeneral Headquarters edict that the ʒentral Solomons was to be held at ll costs, they decided that they ᵥould hold New Guinea with the ocal forces deployed there and direct heir main effort against New Georgia. ᴬs a first step General Imamura ᵥould reinforce the South East De-ached Force with 8,000 men and mmediate action was taken to do his. On the night of 4th July, four ᴶapanese destroyers carried the first nits towards Kolombangara but the ᶠorce encountered Task Force Group ᶾ6.1, which was supporting the north-ʳn landing group, and turned back ᵘt not before a US destroyer, the ᶾtrong, had been sunk by means of a long range torpedo the Japanese navy had developed.

However it was vital to get the men on to Kolombangara if the movement of the greater part of the American Force across to the New Georgia mainland was to be countered, and the following night the Japanese des-troyers set out again. This time there were ten of them and the operation was supervised by Vice-Admiral Samajima who had moved to the Shortlands and wore his flag on the cruiser Chokai. Three ships of the convoy acted as screens for the re-mainder who carried the troops.

The Coastwatchers signal from Vella Lavella had alerted Admiral Halsey and he ordered Admiral Ains-worth with three cruisers (Honolulu, Helena and St Louis) and four des-troyers (Nicholas, O'Bannion, Radford and Jenkins) to intercept. Shortly after midnight, in the Kula Gulf, Admiral Ainsworth's group made contact and by 0330 the Helena and the Japanese destroyers Niizuki and Nagat-suki were either sunk or beached and out of the battle. Only 850 Japanese troops had been landed before the survivors retired. Meanwhile Tokyo's reaction to Admiral Kusaka's request for an additional division of troops was negative. Admiral Kusaka had asked for 2,000 new troops to hold the area of Rice Anchorage, 3,000 for the Munda Airfield, 2,000 to hold a line between the airfield and the Allies and finally a counterattacking force of 4,000 to sweep the Allies off the Munda area and New Georgia. Un-fortunately Admiral Koga, the Com-bined Fleet commander, while be-lieving that the Solomons should be held, considered that the best way to do this was by enticing Admiral Nimitz to commit a large part of the Pacific Fleet under Admiral Halsey's command to the Solomon area. Then the Combined Fleet would destroy the American fleet in piecemeal fashion. Thus Admiral Kusaka was left to defend the New Georgia area without proper reinforcements.

Landings on the New Georgia coasts

On the 4th July 1943, the 2,200 troops of the Northern Landing Group, New Georgia Occupation Force, went aboard a large APD convoy and as dusk fell they moved northwards from Guadalcanal at high speed and the force was landed in the vicinity of Rice Anchorage, a jungle surrounded cove on the north west shore of New Guinea. The intention was to prevent the Japanese on Munda from receiving supplies and reinforcements from their barge bases at Enogai and Bairoko on the Dragon peninsula. Information about the enemy in the area was scanty as patrols had been unable to bring back much worthwhile information and the heavy bush was impenetrable to aerial photography. It was thought that some 500 of the enemy might occupy Bairoko harbour.

The force of 2,200 men was made up of the 1st Raider Regiment US Marines, consisting of the 1st Raider Battalion under Lieutenant-Colonel S B Griffith and the 4th Raider Bat-

talion under Lieutenant-Colonel M S Currin, under the overall command of Colonel H B Liversedge (known as 'Harry the Horse' to his men); in addition there were the 145th Infantry US Army, under Lieutenant-Colonel G G Freer and the 3rd Battalion 148th Infantry US Army under Lieutenant-Colonel D E Schultz. Admiral Turner had ordered Colonel Liversedge to land as secretly as possible at the Pundakona river mouth where it emptied into Rice Anchorage. This anchorage should provide shelter from the weather and be out of sight of Japanese observers on Kolombangara – or so it was hoped. While the APDs moved rapidly toward their objective, Task Force Group 36.2 bombarded Japanese positions in the Vila-Stanmore areas of Kolombangara and the Enogai and Bairoko areas on New Georgia, and were in turn fired upon by concealed Japanese 140mm guns near Enogai Inlet. At least two

Approaching Laiana under fire

of these guns switched their attentions to APDs but without doing any damage. However the element of surprise had been lost and the difficulty of locating the mouth of the Pundakona river in the darkness delayed the landings.

As dawn broke a long range gun on Kolombangara began to shell the shipping which was immobile in the water as landings proceeded so that at 0559 with ten per cent of the stores still to be landed, Colonel Liversedge decided that the ships had been exposed to enemy attack for long enough and radioed the single word 'Scram' in clear. The APDs lost no time in getting under way and leaving Kula Gulf. It was most unfortunate that a high powered communication set which was on board one of the APDs was not unloaded as this led to many difficulties and repercussions later.

On shore the troops contacted Captain Clay Boyd of the 1st Raider Battalion who had with him a Coastwatcher, Flight Lieutenant Corrigan, RAFVR, and his scouts. Despite the

Griffith and Currin (second and third from left) confer on jungle strategy

terrible conditions of rain and mud and tangled undergrowth the scouts led the troops to the assembly areas prepared previously for them and at 0600, operating under radio silence, the troops began their march along three pre-cut trails towards Enogai. However they were without Company I, 148th Infantry which had been landed in error at Kubo Kubo inlet some seven miles to the north and who, under Captain D C Roundtree, were marching as fast as they could to catch up with the parent group. Torrential rain cut communications and runners had to be used for contact between the temporary base on the south bank of the Pundakona river and the advancing troops. At 0800 the 3rd Battalion, 148th Infantry moved directly south to establish a road block on the Munda-Bairoko trail while the remainder of the force headed west and north through a swamp towards the mouth of the Enogai inlet. By nightfall the army and Marine units had reached the south side of the Tamoko river and had to bivouac in a swamp having advanced only about 800 yards, as the crow flies, during the day. It proved impossible to contact Rendova by

radio and the only way for Northern Landing Group signals to reach General Hester was through a monitoring watch kept at Admiral Turner's headquarters which copied all the messages and passed them to General Hester, having to revert to dropping messages by plane if the traffic was heavy. This was another example of the extreme difficulty in communicating from the jungle and in the jungle during the New Georgia campaign. The high humidity and the near impossibility of keeping transmitters and receivers dry were the main reasons for breakdowns.

The South Pacific Scouts who had landed originally at Zenana were much in demand for long range reconnaissance. They knew the jungle and to them there was nothing frightening or unfamiliar about it. The Tongans, Fijians and Solomon Islanders very soon made themselves felt and their score of enemy dead very soon passed their own unit strength of 130. So much use was made of them by the Allied Command that by 7th July the reserve of seventy-five men left at Aola on Guadalcanal was ordered forward. The detachment arrived at a particularly opportune

moment for, just prior to their landing, General Hester's headquarters were suddenly made aware that a group of at least 200 Japanese had infiltrated the Allied lines and was only a mile or so away from the Command Post which was defended by a mixed collection of orderlies, signallers, clerks, cooks etc, as every other available man had been sent forward to help with the drive pressing on towards Munda. Captain David Williams in command of the unit was told to report to the general immediately, and was asked to take over the defence of the Command Post. Williams was given some thirty American service men and his enlarged unit hastily created a fox hole perimeter round the camp almost under the eyes of the Japanese who were little more than one hundred yards away. The Japanese launched their first attack at 1930 and fighting continued throughout the night until 0200 the next day. During that time not a single Japanese managed to get through the perimeter although several of their bodies were found

Fijian 'South Pacific Scouts' are extremely effective in the jungle

on the edges of the defenders' foxholes. In fact one of the enemy had crawled up to a foxhole and whispered in English 'Are you American or Japanese?' He did not live to hear the reply. Williams said afterwards that the Commandos forming his unit had shown a precise and deadly marksmanship – they had been picking off the enemy in the dark at thirty yards range. Dawn revealed thirty-four Japanese dead outside the perimeter and as the enemy had removed their wounded and all the dead they could reach their casualties must have been much heavier than that. The Allies lost one Sergeant killed and one Colonel was wounded. None of the Commandos was touched although some had bullet holes through their jungle green.

The move of General Hester's troops out of the beachhead proceeded very slowly. The weather was one major obstacle but another reason was the extreme caution in the tactics adopted by the troops. After the war General Sasaki, when interrogated, said, 'The rate of speed of the infantry advance was extremely slow. They (the Americans) waited the results of several days of bombardment before a squad advanced'. The infantry appeared to find unusual difficulty in moving towards the Barike river which was the line of departure and as the two regiments went forward. the 169th Infantry operating inland through heavy jungle on the right fell behind the 172nd, which was advancing along the coast to the west, and it was through the gap thus created that the hostile raid which Captain Williams and his men had stopped had been launched.

By the 7th July the forward elements of both regiments had reached the river but only the 172nd Regiment was ready to begin the attack and General Hester, anxious to get the attack moving, ordered Lieutenant Blake to bring up the Marine tanks to Zenana the next day and then proceed forward to spearhead the advance. The next two days were spent preparing for the assault and at 0300 on 9th July one of the heaviest artillery barrages of the Pacific war was laid down as a preparation prior to the assault. About this episode General Sasaki said: 'The enemy with complete material superiority shelled and bombed us heavily night and day, and at the same time added naval fire to this. Enemy laid waste the battlefield and then ordered an infantry advance.'

The two regiments of the 43rd Division moved off on schedule but such was the exhaustion engendered by reaching the line of departure that their efforts lacked energy and aggressiveness thus preventing the proper use of patrols for procuring vital intelligence. This lack of aggression also allowed the enemy to close in on the American lines and they were so close that they avoided the shelling and were able to meet the American attacks.

General Hester now realised that if he could secure a beach-head at Laiana it would shorten his supply route considerably and help to relieve a situation in which the 169th Infantry, now only 3,000 yards from its original landing point, had fallen far behind the 172nd on its left and both regiments were still out of contact with one another so that small groups of Japanese found it easy to infiltrate between them and harass their flanks, lines of communications and rear installations. Added to which snooper planes at night prevented the exhausted troops from getting their sleep and General Sasaki's effective use of his 90mm mortars, which he fired into the American forces whenever he was shelled by their artillery made the Americans believe they were being shelled by their own guns.

By the night of 12th July, the 172nd were still too far from Laiana to launch an assault the next morning, and it was not until dusk on 13th that the tired regiment reached the Laiana area and then were too fatigued to do more than dig themselves in for the

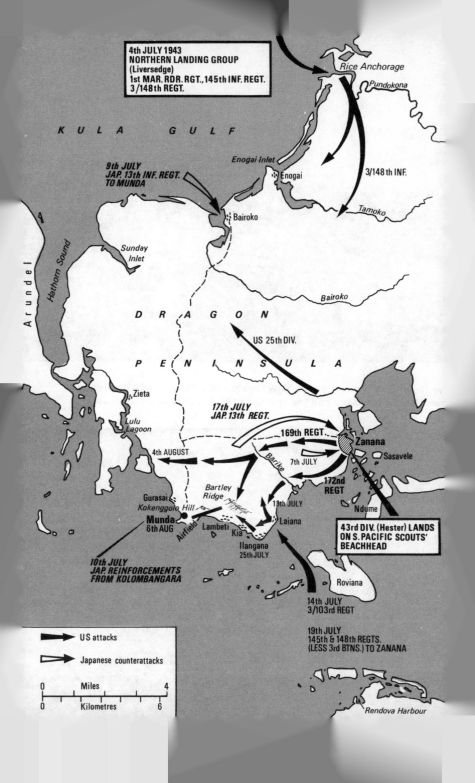

4th JULY 1943
NORTHERN LANDING GROUP
(Liversedge)
1st MAR. RDR. RGT., 145th INF. REGT.
3/148th REGT.

Rice Anchorage

Pundokona

K U L A   G U L F

9th JULY
JAP. 13th INF. REGT.
TO MUNDA

Enogai Inlet

Enogai

3/148 th INF.

Bairoko

Tamoko

A
r
u
n
d
e
l

H
a
t
h
o
r
n

S
o
u
n
d

*Sunday
Inlet*

Bairoko

D   R   A   G   O   N

US 25th DIV.

P   E   N   I   N   S   U   L   A

,Zieta

17th JULY
JAP. 13th REGT.

169th REGT.

*Lulu
Lagoon*

4th AUGUST

Barike

7th JULY

Zanana

Sasavele

**172nd
REGT**

*Bartley
Ridge*

13th JULY

Gurasai
Kokenggolo Hill

Munda
6th AUG

Airfield

Lambeti

Kia

Laiana

Ndume

43rd DIV. (Hester) LANDS
ON S. PACIFIC SCOUTS'
BEACHHEAD

Ilangana
25th JULY

10th JULY
JAP. REINFORCEMENTS
FROM KOLOMBANGARA

Roviana

14th JULY
3/103rd REGT

19th JULY
145th & 148th REGTS.
(LESS 3rd BTNS.) TO ZANANA

US attacks

Japanese counterattacks

| 0 | Miles | 4 |

| 0 | Kilometres | 6 |

Rendova Harbour

Above: Infantry storm ashore on New Georgia having crossed from Rendova
Below: Halsey, Griswold and Senator Cabot Lodge visit forward areas

night. General Sasaki took immediate advantage of the situation and sent in the 3rd Battalion of the 13th Japanese Infantry Regiment to exploit the gap between the American lines. At 0800 on 14th July, the 172nd began to move towards Ilangana and as they did so landing craft took the 3rd Battalion 103rd Regiment and Marine tanks to Laiana. The infantry and tanks went ashore with only minor resistance from the enemy and the 9th Defence Battalion's special weapons group set up their weapons for anti-aircraft defence on the beach-head. Inland however the tale was one of woe as the 172nd, moving forward very slowly, was eventually pinned down from prepared enemy positions sited on a steep hill. Nearer the beach very strong opposition from well sited and hidden strong points was encountered, so much so that on both flanks the attack ground to a halt. The situation was now serious and did not please Halsey at all.

General Harmon was ordered to examine the situation, find out what was wrong and take immediate steps to rectify matters. He accordingly investigated the positions of all concerned with great thoroughness and instructed General Griswold, the XIV Corps Commander, to assume control of the New Georgia Occupation Force. By this time a large part of two divisions from General Griswold's corps – the 43rd and the 37th were committed to operation TOENAILS and indeed some of them were already engaged in the front line, and it was logical that Griswold should command them. Moreover this would release General Hester to devote himself full time to his own division. At the same time Rear Admiral Wilkinson would replace Admiral Turner as Commander CTF 31 on 15th July. This move had been planned many months before.

The fight for the Central Solomons was never centred in any one area; instead there were many actions in progress almost simultaneously and some of these involved new tactics and new weapons. It was here that the Allies scored because they did not hesitate to improvise as and when necessary, whereas the enemy always followed the orders laid down for them even if they resulted in their own annihilation. They showed no flexi-

Vice-Admiral Theodore S Wilkinson who replaced Turner

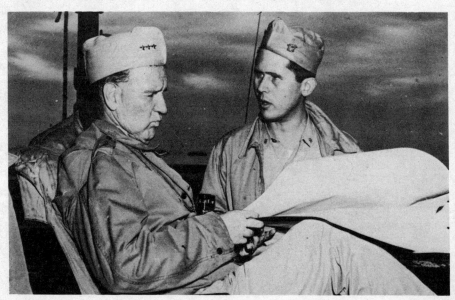

The M3A1 'General Stuart' light tank was the first US tank of the Second World War to see action, and continued in service in the Far East long after it had been replaced by later models in the West, as a result of the poor types of anti-tank weapons possessed by the Japanese, and the peculiar terrain of such areas as New Guinea, where small size and manoeuvrability were more important than heavy armour and a more powerful armament. *Weight:* 12.7 tons. *Crew:* four. *Armament:* one M6 L/57 37mm gun with 111 rounds and three .3-inch Browning machine guns with 7,000 rounds. *Speed:* 36mph maximum. *Maximum gradient:* 26 degrees. *Fording depth:* 3½ feet. *Turning radius:* 26 feet. *Range:* 60 miles maximum. *Length:* 14 feet 10 inches. *Width:* 7 feet 6 inches. *Height:* 7 feet 4 inches. *Engine:* one Continental W-670 petrol engine, 250hp. *Armour:* 2 inches lower front and turret front, 1½ inches turret sides and rear and driver's front, 1 inch sides and lower rear, ½ inch lower nose, ¾ inch upper rear, ⅜ inch deck, floor and turret top

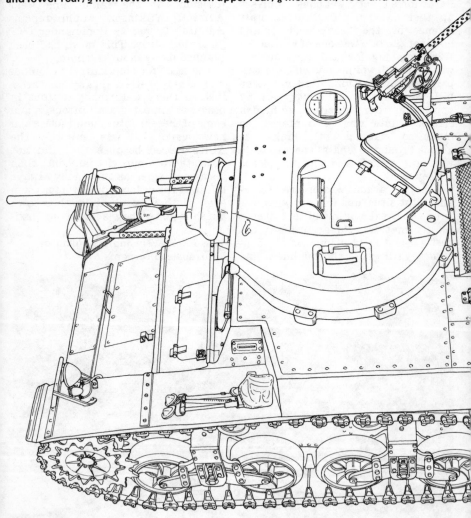

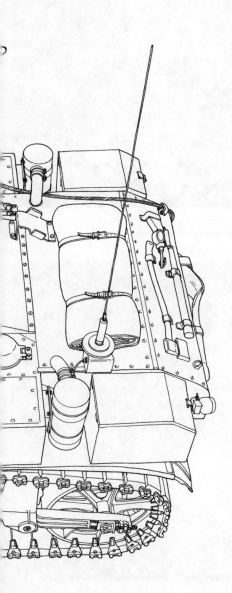

bility in any sector of their commands and suffered accordingly. The use of Marine tanks in thick jungle illustrated the effectiveness of the Allied approach to new problems – tanks had never before been used in jungle but the Allies were willing to try them out – and a considerable success they proved to be.

On 15th July Captain Blake of the Marine Defence Battalion sent a tank platoon from the Zenana beachead inland to the 3rd Battalion Command Post in order to support its attacks while Captain Blake took another tank platoon inland to the 2nd Battalion for the same purpose. Six infantry men were assigned to each tank to give it close protection and Solomon Islanders were provided as guides. After advancing about one hundred yards from the front lines the leading tanks came on an open space and seeing enemy bunkers they fanned out and began firing high explosive and canister ammunition into the enemy's defences. This attack flushed out a number of Japanese who were shot at by the accompanying infantry but the thick jungle prevented proper sighting of their targets and the men were in danger of losing sight of the tanks. Then an enemy machine gun opened up and hit the hatch of the leading tank but caused no casualties. The range was so close that the periscopes were impeded by parallax between their guns and themselves and matters were not helped by the smoke from the 37mm guns which prevented observation of the impact area of the projectiles. Gradually the bunkers were reduced and it was discovered later that the Japanese who kept appearing to take the place of their comrades shot down by tanks and infantry were members of a tank killer unit sent forward to disable the tanks with flame throwers and magnetic mines. Finally the tank machine guns gave the area a general raking and the supporting infantry moved in and occupied the extreme left of the Japanese beach defences covering their

Battle-stained tank crew relax on their return from a mission

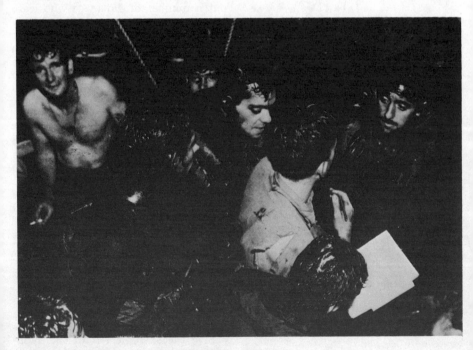

Survivors of *USS Helena* after the Battle of Kula Gulf

zone of the Munda area. However there remained, to be discovered later, many well constructed and hidden bunkers which caused a great deal of trouble to the 103rd Infantry when XIV Corps began its July offensive.

The other tank platoon under Gunnery Sergeant Spurlock had reached the foot of the hill facing the advance of the 3rd Battalion. This had five well concealed bunkers on its forward slope and the tanks attacked at once aided by tracer fire from the accompanying infantry. An intense fire fight developed with grenades and anti tank mines being hurled at the tanks but they failed to make much impression and the bunkers were soon reduced to allow the infantry to move in to hold the new position.

Next day the tank platoons rejoined the units with which they had been operating and pressed forward inland to win a hill two hundred yards beyond the previous day's objective. But on the coast where Captain Blake made two sorties unsupported by infantry, all the good work done on that day up to 1600 was of no avail because there was no way of preventing the Japanese from getting too close to the tanks for their fire power to be effective, nor could they make sure that a bunker which had been reduced could be held against the enemy. However that evening the 145th Infantry began to relieve the 169th and the 3rd Battalion, 103rd Infantry replaced the 2nd Battalion, 172nd Infantry. Next morning the attack was resumed at 1000. On 17th July, Captain Blake received orders to take his remaining tanks and support Company I which was encountering stiff resistance from a large thicket a short distance from the beach. The tanks went forward and plunged into the thicket and bullets began to bounce off them like hail from a roof. The Japanese attacked with flame throwers and grenades and one magnetic mine slapped on the base of a turret stove in the hull and wounded two men in one of the tanks. The bush was now swarming with the enemy where previously there had been friendly troops and there was nothing for it but to retire. A cable was attached to the disabled tank under heavy fire and it was towed back, protected by the remaining tanks, and the platoon fought its way back to the American lines reaching them by 1400. Captain Blake was then informed that the attack was to be discontinued until next day. Although the infantry-tank combined operation was in its infancy there was enough evidence to show that it was likely to develop into a most effective weapon in thick jungle so long as the ground was firm enough to take the weight of the tanks.

It was about this time that the end of the saga that had started as the battle of Kula Gulf on 6th July took place. The USS Helena had been damaged and subsequently this American light cruiser sank in the Kula gulf but a large number of the crew had taken to the boats and life rafts and the winds and currents had drifted them across to the north west coast of Vella Lavella. They were contacted immediately on landing by the Coastwatchers and taken inland to safety. Lieutenants Josselyn and Firth, with the help of Dr Silvester at Biloa mission, brought the 175 men to safety under the very noses of the Japanese patrols on the island and in many cases the scouts brought men through the enemy camps without losing a single man during the ten days the men were on the island. Josselyn and Firth were very hard put to it to feed, clothe and attend to the medical needs of the men but when, on 16th July, destroyers arrived off the south-east coast at night to pick up the men not one had been lost and the evacuation, mounted in the dark under conditions of extreme difficulty, was carried out successfully. Again the courage and skill of the islanders was outstanding and their care and shepherding of the sailors and marines from the Helena could not have been bettered.

Japanese counterattack

The only reinforcements to be sent to the aid of Admiral Kusaka and General Imamura were the 21st Air Flotilla consisting of twenty fighters, twelve attack planes, two reconnaissance planes and the aircraft carrier *Ryuho*'s air group of twenty-five fighters and twenty-eight light bombers. These arrived on 2nd July and five days later Admiral Koga sent three cruisers and three destroyers to Rabaul to support Admiral Samejima's 8th Fleet. Admiral Kusaka had already made attempts to attack American shipping and ground positions and in doing so a considerable proportion of his air strength had been lost. Now the tide of battle was such that he had to continue to reinforce Admiral Ota and General Sasaka in the Central Solomons without having sufficient means to be able to do so in a satisfactory manner.

On the night of 9th July 1,200 Japanese troops were landed on Kolombangara Island and on the same night 1,300 men of the Japanese 13th Infantry moved from Kolombangara to Bairoko and then overland to Munda and there reported to General Sasaki. They were followed the next night by the 1,200 who had landed on 9th July. The Coast-watchers reported these movements but at that time the Allies were in no position to counter the moves. One battalion of the 13th reinforced the defence of the Dragon Peninsula by joining up with the Kure 6th SNLF and finally, on the night of 12th-13th July, a further 1,200 Japanese landed on Kolombangara (this group had been carried by the convoy which later met US Task Force 18 in the battle for Kolombangara, losing its flagship *Jintsu* while the Allies lost the destroyer *Gwin*; the cruisers *Honolulu, St Louis* and *HMNZS Leander* being damaged).

General Sasaki had now deployed the main body of the 229th Infantry and also the 13th, the 7th SNLF and some troops from the 230th Infantry who had served previously on Guadalcanal. He

The devastation at Munda

had already interposed a battalion of the 13th Infantry between the American 172nd and the 169th Regiments and his plan for the major battle appeared simple on paper. The 13th Infantry were to swing wide to the north east and engulf the Allied right flank, cut the Munda trail between the front and Zenana beach, then destroy the 169th. At the same time the 3rd battalion, 229th Infantry would attack the 2nd Battalion 172nd Infantry while the SNLF would infiltrate from the beaches west of Laiana Beach, destroying General Hester's beach defences and cutting supply lines and communications along the shore. Meanwhile the remainder of the 229th would be held near Lambeti plantation ready to exploit any advantage or defend the position against Allied counterattacks.

The snags which arose to hinder the execution of this plan were the jungle and the terrain both of which bedevilled movement impartially whether it was Japanese or Allied. Especially were the effects felt in the matter of communication either by radio or by runner (any runner was soon reduced to a stumbling, sliding, foot slogging progress). The 13th Infantry set out for their three day march through the mud and thick jungle to turn the right flank of the 169th and at the same time patrols from the 229th became increasingly active making minor attacks up and down the position of the so called 'front.' The Japanese holding the bunkers, part of the SNLF, continued to cling to them tenaciously despite very heavy artillery and mortar fire and, on 17th July, General Sasaki began his attack but a breakdown in his communications prevented co-ordination. Heavy Allied attacks on the 3rd Battalion put them off balance and they could not launch their initial drive while air strikes and artillery bombardment so disrupted the boat pool from which the SNLF

USS Honolulu at Tulagi displays her damaged bows

were to have infiltrated behind General Hester's beachhead at Laiana that their attack never started. However the 13th Japanese Infantry were able to turn the right flank of the American 43rd Division and by 1600 on 17th July they were poised on the banks of the Barike river, and at sundown the attack against the Zenana beach supply dumps and the 43rd Division command post was launched. Within a few minutes the command post, which was on the shore about 400 yards west of Zenana beach, had been surrounded and the supply lines leading to the front and rear had been cut.

Fortunately one telephone line had been overlooked and the Americans were able to call for artillery support from Roviana and Sasavele islands. The guns of the 43rd Division responded promptly and effectively and General Barker, their commander, himself acted as one of the forward observers. Box barrages and accurate shelling some one-hundred yards forward of the American positions kept the enemy off throughout the night and prevented them organising 'banzai' charges. On Zenana beach, however, which was protected by the 3rd Platoon, Special Weapons group of the Marine Corps, under Lieutenant Wismer, things were far from comfortable. Lieutenant Wismer realised that if the Japanese captured the beachhead they would also capture a large proportion of the American supplies on New Georgia and the primary landing point for men and material. His plan, rapidly devised, was to man his 20mm and 40mm guns with half the usual number of men and use the others to set up positions on a hill about 150 yards inland overlooking a trail which ran to the command post and along which the enemy were almost sure to come. Two light machine guns were salvaged from the 172nd

Left: HMNZS Leander. Below: front to rear, USSs O'Bannon, Chevalier and Taylor

Infantry dump and hastily the platoon dug in on the sides of the knoll. To their right was the 172nd Infantry anti tank platoon and to their left about fifty Army Service troops and artillerymen. A perimeter defence was set up and the newly acquired machine guns, manned by Corporal Rothschild and Private Wantuck, were sighted in to fire down the critical trail.

At about 2100 a group of about one-hundred Japanese came into the defile below the hill and started to set up mortars. The defenders held their fire until the number of Japanese round the mortars was at its maximum and then opened up. The Japanese fled into the jungle, regrouped and made a 'banzai' charge which overran the Marine defenders who then made their way individually back to the gun positions on the beach where they prepared to make a last stand. But no attack came.

At first light, after a tense night during which the few remaining men stood to in anticipation of further Japanese attacks, Lieutenant Wismer regrouped his men and led them back to the hill where they found the reason for the silence and non activity during the night. Corporal Rothschild and Private Wantuck had stayed with their guns and the dead Japanese who littered the hill were evidence of the effect of their fire and the hand to hand knife and grenade fighting which had followed. Private Wantuck was dead and Corporal Rothschild, badly wounded, was found under some brush in a nearby gully. Both men were recommended for Medals of Honour, the highest American award but in the event they were decorated with the Navy Cross. It may well have been the bravery and determination of these two men alone which saved Zenana Beach and prevented the disruption of the American supply route to New Georgia.

All was not well with the 169th and the 172nd Regiments. The 169th had expended a great deal of energy in its wide swing to the right and was now too exhausted to advance further and the 172nd had come to a halt along its sector of the front with its effective strength fifty per cent below normal. Malaria, lack of communications, mud, and the jungle frustrated both regiments and the constant air attacks by the enemy (eighty in the first twenty days), while doing little damage, had adverse effects on the troops' nerves and physical endurance since they were unable to sleep. The once eager troops had little will to fight and the 'front line' became static. This was not a situation which could be tolerated by the Allies and on the morning of 18th July, the 148th Infantry (less its 3rd Battalion) commanded by Major-General R S Beightler landed at Zenana Beach and immediately began the relief of the 172nd. On 19th its sister regiment, the 145th (less its 3rd Battalion) took over from the 169th. The 172nd and the 169th Regiments were moved to the left to cover that front and by 23rd July General Griswold had two divisions on a 4,000-yard front and was still some two miles short of the XIV Corps objective.

In making plans for the future assault two things became clear. One was that the Marine tanks were most effective in spear-heading assaults because they were comparatively impervious to small arms fire and had armament which could deal directly with the many and well hidden bunkers which the enemy had created. The second was that the tanks could not operate efficiently unless they were supported by infantry men armed with flame throwers, grenades and other weapons which could be used to protect the tanks against close quarter attack and also to flush out enemy bunkers and prevent the enemy re-occupying them when the tanks had passed on. There was also the perpetual need to guard against anti-tank mines planted on or very near the tank 'blind spots'.

On the morning of 24th July five

Marine tanks were ordered to spearhead the attack from the centre of the left zone of action. Following a three hour artillery barrage which left enemy positions largely untouched (as the infantry soon found out) the tanks moved forward to engage the Japanese holding out on a large hill. The attack crept slowly ahead against very heavy Japanese fire and by 1400 mechanical failures and minor damage from enemy fire forced three of the five Marine tanks to withdraw before the hill was overrun. But the barrage of fire from the Allies had proved too much for the defenders and with the two undamaged machines continuing to move forward, the infantry were able to advance and take the hill.

The left wing of the XIV Corps was 500 yards behind the right wing and General Griswold decided that the advance of both wings must be together and not in a 'stepped' configuration which allowed the enemy to penetrate. As a prelude to rectifying this position a heavy preliminary bombardment was carried out on 25th July. At 0005 hours seven destroyers and later 171 planes of various types began bombarding the Munda area. 145 tons of bombs were dropped and hundreds of 5-inch shells from the destroyers swept the area. The advance then began. The first check came near to the beach where a Japanese strongpoint held up the advance and to reduce this the 2nd Battalion of the 172nd swung first north and then south to face the lagoon and the tanks of the 9th Defence Battalion USMC moved forward supported by a fresh and experienced infantry company.

At noon an artillery barrage was put down on known and suspected Japanese bunkers and positions and at 1300 the fire was lifted and the tanks, closely followed by the riflemen, rumbled forward. The Japanese abandoned their emplacements and ran for cover leaving the 47mm anti-tank guns

Front line command post conference, General Beightler at left

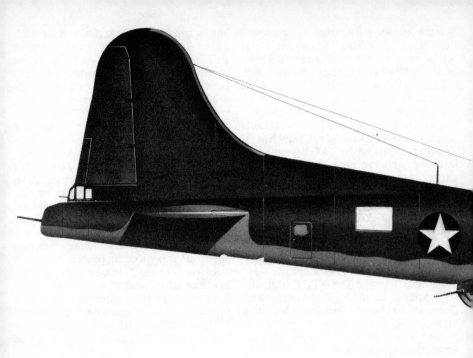

which had caused so much damage earlier to be taken by the infantry who then mopped up the stragglers. As soon as the ground was cleared troops from the 3rd Battalion 103rd Infantry fanned out and occupied the Ilangana peninsula. This co-ordination of tanks, artillery and infantry had worked very well and ensured success – the emphasis being on the word co-ordination.

On 26th and 27th July, the six tanks of the 10th Marine Defence Battalion led an assault on Bartley ridge, a hill feature 800 yards long stretching across the front of the XIV Corps right wing. Behind them the 103rd Infantry on the left advanced to shorten and straighten the front line which, at that time, slanted from southeast to northwest. The tanks were deployed in two lines of three each with eighteen infantry-men armed with flame throwers, automatic weapons, rifles and grenades as close escorts. However the Japa-nese had anticipated the type of attack

which was to be thrust on them and soon after leaving the Allied front line enfilading fire drove off the infantry support from each tank to such an extent that a Japanese marine managed to climb on the back of a tank and fix a magnetic mine to the hull. He was killed by machine gun fire from the other tanks but not be-fore his mine had exploded knocking out the Marine tank before it had really got started. The other tanks carried on until, entering a clearing they found themselves surrounded by cleverly sited pill boxes and bunkers and subjected to heavy fire. This they returned and fighting continued for five hours during which one tank got stuck and despite efforts to tow it free it was not possible to do so. Ammuni-tion and fuel were running low so First Lieutenant Bailey, the tank com-mander, ordered a withdrawal. One tank lost its way and was destroyed and a second arrived back in the tank

A development of the B-17E, the Boeing B-17F heavy bomber could be recognised by its new clear plastic nose, which carried mountings for additional defensive guns, and more powerful engines. *Engines:* four Wright R-1820 radials, 1,200hp each at 25,000 feet. *Armament:* up to twelve Browning .5-inch machine guns as defensive armament, plus an offensive bomb load of up to 8,000 lbs. *Speed:* 299mph at 25,000 feet. *Ceiling:* 37,500 feet. *Range:* 1,300 miles with a 6,000 lbs of bombs, 2,880 maximum. *Climb:* 25.7 minutes to 25,000 feet. *Weight empty/loaded:* 34,000/56,500 lbs. *Span:* 103 feet 9 inches. *Length:* 74 feet 9 inches

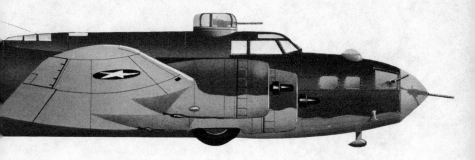

park only after a long and circuitous detour.

The three remaining tanks took on fuel and returned to the scene of the battle but were met with such a concentration of fire that Bailey realised that to rescue the two badly damaged tanks would probably cause destruction of the other three and again withdrew. That night American artillery and mortars laid down a semi continuous barrage in the area and next morning, when Bailey returned to the area, he found one tank damaged beyond repair and destroyed it with an incendiary grenade and the other was later towed back to safety.

The attack on 26th July was only partially successful although the 103rd Infantry managed to break through to Kia village after dealing with a line of bunkers in depth. The right flank was still ahead of the left and it was more important to bring up the left by advancing along the shore than driving

further forward on the right which could contain the enemy opposite it for the time being. General Griswold decided to move on the left and ordered the 3rd Battalion, 103rd Infantry supported by the 9th Defence Battalion of the Marine Corps to strike at Lambeti Plantation the next day.

Again a combination of heavy jungle and well hidden and expertly handled anti-tank guns brought to bear by the enemy dealt severe damage to the tanks, five of which were knocked out, while the infantry could not advance. However, as a counter measure the heavy American fire and artillery support proved so severe that the enemy were forced eventually to withdraw leaving well sited machine guns and a damaged 47mm anti-tank gun. The Marine Defence Battalion were now in a somewhat parlous state with eight tanks out of action, four permanently.

By 28th July, XIV Corps had made some progress but it was not until

Dead Japanese sprawls amid the ruins of a fortified tunnel entrance.

Major-General Hodge flanked by Brigadier-Generals Sebree and Woodward

First US plane to land on the repaired Munda airstrip

General Hester sent forward Brigadier-General Wing to the command post of the 3rd Battalion, 103rd Infantry with instructions to plan and conduct an attack by that battalion that the situation improved. First the general insisted that the tanks must be given close support and that each tank should be escorted by one flame thrower, two automatic rifles and six riflemen armed with incendiary and fragmentation grenades. The tanks must be closely followed by a rifle company and a heavy weapons company so that the ground they won should not be retaken by the enemy. All concerned were briefed on the plan and after a thirty minute artillery and mortar preparation the tanks and their escorts advanced together.

Very heavy opposition was encountered but strong support by the accompanying troops broke up the mine attacks on the tanks and the combined action soon succeeded in taking the forty log and coral shelters which lay across the axis of the advance. This assault went forward for 500 yards and although the tanks penetrated another quarter of a mile there were insufficient infantrymen to mop up and occupy the additional ground. The action had proved that even tired troops could compare with fresh ones when properly handled and with good leadership, for the attack had taken what was the strongest point on the main enemy line of resistance.

On 29th July Major-General J R Hodge replaced General Hester as commander of the 43rd Division, and one week later Munda airfield was captured by the Allies. XIV Corps, much encouraged by the breakthrough on 28th July, continued to make daily advances westward of the order of 500 to 1,200 yards and by the 4th August they had reached Lulu Lagoon 600 yards north of Gurasai in the Kindu area. The remaining defenders in the Munda area were now encircled in an area measuring about 1,000 yards by 1,400 yards and since they could no longer be reinforced, it was thought by the Allied Command that they would attempt a withdrawal by night. But again the Allies had not reckoned on the stubborness of the Japanese and their defence of Bibilo and Kokegolo Hills continued unbated and it was not until the remaining tanks of the 10th Defence Battalion had succeeded in knocking out the anti-tank and other guns with which the hills were defended, that the infantry were able to assault and take the hills. Even so many Japanese had retired into the caves under Kokegolo hill and since they would not surrender the mouths of the caves were dynamited in and they were left to die.

At 1500 on 5th August Griswold reported to Halsey that organised resistance in the area of Munda had ceased and that mopping up operations were in progress while the badly damaged landing strip was being put in order. At the time Griswold had 30,000 troops available divided into seven combat teams all of whom had contributed in some measure to the completion of the TOENAILS operation but it is significant that against the American numbers, the Japanese had only about 8,000 men and yet by their courage and skill they held up the Allied forces far longer than had been anticipated. This situation was also due to the fact that in some units of the Allied forces the leadership and state of training left much to be desired.

Meanwhile the 25th Division had been working its slow way northwest through the jungle and swamp on the Munda-Bairoko trail in order to cut the retreat and supply route of any of the enemy remaining on New Georgia and to mop up any strongpoints that might be found. On 9th August, the 1st Battalion 27th Infantry contacted patrols of the Northern Landing Force and finally, in a co-ordinated drive on 24th August, units of the 25th and 37th Division took Bairoko thus ending the campaign on New Georgia Island.

The drive on the north coasts

On 7th July, the combined forces of the 1st Marine Raider Battalion, 1st Raider Regiment Headquarters and Companies K and L, 145th Infantry moved wetly and wearily out of the swamp in which they had spent the night and began to march towards Enogai. The villages of Maranusa I, Triri and Maranusa II lay across the trail, which was very narrow and tortuous close to the base of a steep coral ridge running parallel to the Tamoko river, and with Company D and Solomon Island scouts leading, the force moved in on Maranusa I to find it undefended without bunkers or other installations, although there were signs of recent occupation.

After a thorough exploration of the area with negative results the leading patrol pushed on and some twenty minutes later bumped into a seven man Japanese patrol which was immediately attacked. This attack resulted in the death of two Japanese and the wounding of the remaining five. Inspection showed that they had belonged to the 782 strong Kure 6th SNLF responsible for the protection of the Enogai barge base. Colonel Liversedge assumed rightly that the shooting would have alerted other Japanese forces in the area and sent the 1st Raider Battalion ahead under Lieutenant-Colonel Griffith to meet any attacks which might develop. At 1230 the Solomon Islanders attached to the Raider Battalion saw a Japanese patrol of about company size approaching and after a preliminary exchange of shots the companies of the Raider Battalion moving to the left and right of the opposing force compelled them to withdraw, leaving behind ten dead and one wounded while three Marines were killed and four wounded. Documents captured revealed amongst other things the defences of Enogai in detail. Colonel Liversedge immediately asked for an air attack on Enogai but it proved

New Georgia veteran, Lloyd Culuck, takes a break

impossible to get through to base on normal channels and it was not until an army station on New Georgia had picked up the message and relayed it, that it reached Guadalcanal. The Allied forces then moved into Maranusa I and Triri and set up defence perimeters for the night while the medical officers cared for the wounded and the dead were buried.

The 3rd Battalion 148th Infantry, who were blocking the Munda-Bairoko trail to the south, discovered on the same day that they were in the wrong position – a very easy error to make in the featureless jungle – and moved forward, but it was not until 1715 that they were in their proper position and it was then too late to install the trail block that night. The block was set up the next morning but meanwhile a message was sent back to Colonel Liversedge asking for supplies of food and ammunition. These were despatched by means of the islanders who were attached to the Raider Regiment under the command of Flight-Lieutenant Corrigan, RAFVR, the Coastwatcher attached to Colonel Liversedge.

Lieutenant-Colonel Griffith, in command of the 1st Raider Battalion decided to set traps for any of the enemy who might approach Triri and at first light he ordered the 1st Platoon of Company B to set an ambush 800 yards down the path towards Bairoko, and a platoon of Company D to prepare an ambush 800 yards from Triri towards Enogai. Some thirty minutes after getting into position at 0630 the platoon from Company D sighted a company of Japanese marching at ease towards Triri. Unfortunately the surprise was spoilt by some trigger happy Marine loosing off too soon and the enemy fell back in good order, regrouped and launched an attack in which Lieutenant Broderick was wounded. The news of this reached Colonel Liversedge by runner and he brought up his command post plus the two reserve companies. Company B was not in-

volved and was withdrawn for support and action elsewhere.

Company D's remaining platoons went to the support of their first platoon and a fight developed in which Company D became disorganised and had to be relieved by Company C. This was done to such effect that the enemy broke contact and retired in the direction of Bairoko leaving approximately fifty dead and by noon the front was quiet, allowing the 1st Raider Battalion to comb the jungle in search of a path through to Enogai. However, the many tracks were very confusing and Lieutenant-Colonel Griffith decided to withdraw his patrols and to cut his way to Enogai along high ground the next day.

By this time the enemy had regrouped and were sending out small parties to discover the American positions and by 1600 the enemy had some 400 men south west of the Triri perimeter and as the 1st Raider Battalion moved back towards Triri, the Japanese struck at the thinly held lines near the junction of Companies K and L and caused disorganisation. Colonel Liversedge ordered a counterattack and this was done through the 1st Platoon of the battalion which moved north along the shores of the Enogai inlet then turned inland and attacked the remaining Japanese causing them to break off the action and retreat towards Bairoko leaving twenty dead in front of the American lines with no casualties to the Marines. The Japanese made no further attempts to take Triri.

That morning at 1105 the 3rd Battalion had cut the enemy's telephone cable and two hours later a Japanese repair party stumbled on the ambush which had been prepared. There was scattered firing and the enemy retreated but at 1500 the Japanese attacked in strength but without much success since they lost at least seven dead compared with the killing of one Marine and the wounding of six others. The enemy then broke off the attack and moved towards Bairoko.

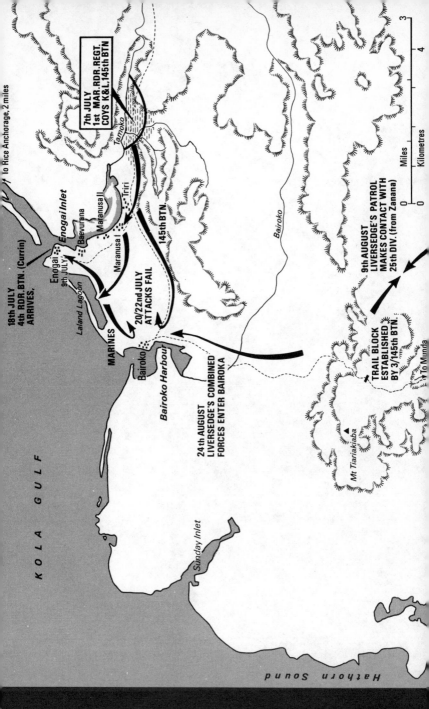

Northern Landing Group takes Engai and Baitoko

Infantry make for the front

Fording a creek on the Munda trail

The Coastwatcher's scouts reported that the Japanese had strong-points in the villages of Maranusa II, Baekinera and Beavurana and so Lieutenant Griffith ordered the 1st Raider Battalion to by-pass the villages. The battalion then reached Laland lagoon and at 1100 turned right and moving to the north they encountered the first enemy outpost outside Enogai. The Raiders advanced against rifle and machine gun fire until 1730 and then dug in for the night. Fortunately the enemy did not take advantage of their favourable position for the 1st Raiders were between the enemy at Enogai and Bairoko. Things were not made easier for Griffith by concern for the position of Lieutenant-Colonel Schultz with his army unit at the end of a long track, and the shortage of food and the poor reserve position added to his worries. The radios were being badly affected by the humidity but by dint of superhuman efforts arrangements were made for a food

Minor casualties – out of the battle for a time

drop the next day.

All units of the 1st Raider Battalion were concerned in the series of fierce little actions which culminated in the taking of Enogai village. Before dawn a patrol from Company B scouted the banks of the inlet to see what kind of terrain would be met along the axis of the proposed advance. The patrol returned at 0600 to report favourably and the attack was mounted with Companies A, C and B from left to right and Company D in reserve. The battalion's 60mm mortars pounded the area ahead and then the battalion moved forward at 0700 under long range overhead machine gun fire which however was ineffective in the zone of attack in front of Company B owing to the thick jungle. Captain Wheeler therefore brought the mortars to bear and these enabled Company B to advance against sporadic resistance to take Baekineru after killing twelve or more Japanese and capturing one heavy and five light machine guns. Companies A and C on more level ground moved slowly forward in the face of severe resis-

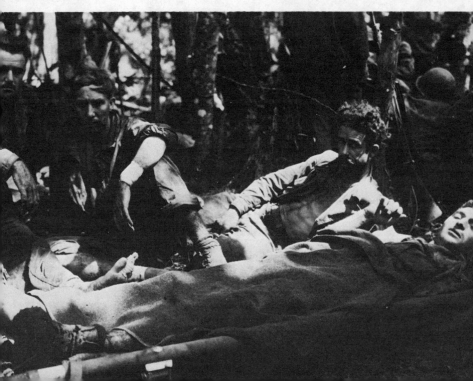

tance and Griffith sent forward one platoon from Company D to exploit the advance of Company B and with mortar shells bursting ahead of them the Marines stormed Enogai village. The Japanese fled, trying to swim to small islands offshore under the withering fire. One pocket of resistance in front of Company A held out until 1500 and then was taken and the enemy in Enogai had ceased to be. As though to reward the victory the food drop arranged the day before had been carried out that morning and supplies reached Enogai shortly before the final mopping up. To men who had been fighting continuously for nearly thirty hours it was welcome indeed. Beach defences were established and Company D, while moving into position, had a short hard fight with a pocket of the enemy with the result that twenty Marines were wounded.

Colonel Liversedge, having established radio contact informed General Hester that Enogai had been taken and asked for several Catalina flying boats to be sent next day to fly out the wounded, but the control station of the net refused to accept the message despite the fact that it was urgent. Finally Liversedge reached someone with some sense and the flight was arranged. This absurd situation highlighted another of the difficulties which should never have arisen between units of the same nation striving towards the same goal. As a result communications between the US Army, Navy and Marines were improved.

Although the taking of Enogai reduced the pressure on the Northern Landing Group to some extent, it still left the problems of reinforcing the Munda-Bairoko trail block which had been forced from its advantageous hill position, and there was also the problem of the capture of Bairoko. Colonel Liversedge ordered Company I of the 145th Regiment to reinforce the road block and except for a small machine gun detachment left at Rice Anchorage, the rest of the force moved up to Enogai.

Marines carry the remains of dead comrades to the graveyard at Enogai

Next day the Japanese launched an air attack which was to be the precursor of almost daily attacks and because a number of Marines were caught out in the open three were killed and fifteen wounded. That afternoon the Catalinas asked for by Colonel Liversedge landed off Enogai and while loading the wounded men they were attacked by Japanese float planes. The Marines on the beach replied with every weapon they could muster and the planes were driven off but not before the Catalinas were damaged. Eventually one hundred sick and wounded men were evacuated and as the other units in the force were suffering from exhaustion, Liversedge asked Admiral Turner to send forward the 4th Marine Raider Battalion.

While waiting for reinforcements and further supplies, which included a powerful TBW radio and its operators, the Northern Landing Force made its preparations for the coming assault on Bairoko but there was the problem of the 3rd Battalion, 145th Infantry which was holding the trail block between Munda and Bairoko. They had been under intermittent attack for some time and despite the addition of Company I, of the 145th, Lieutenant-Colonel Schultz considered that he would be unable to hold his position without further reinforcement. On 13th July Company L of the 145th Infantry was sent down to the trail block following Liversedge who was making a personal reconnaissance. The situation he found was disheartening. In theory Schultz commanded six companies, but sickness, the lack of food and continual skir-

Originally envisaged as an offensive floatplane fighter to give cover to Japanese surface forces during island landings, the Nakajima A6M2-N (codenamed RUFE by the Allies) was basically a standard Mitsubishi A6M Zero fighter. Work on the conversion began early in 1941, the prototype first flying in December of that year and production starting in April 1942. Though the RUFE retained much of its original's superlative manoeuvrability, the floats reduced its performance to a level where true offensive fighter operations were out of the question. The RUFE was then relegated to defensive duties on islands too small to accomodate airfields. Despite its obsolescence, the RUFE was brought out of retirement as a training aircraft to fly as a front-line machine over the Japanese homeland at the end of the

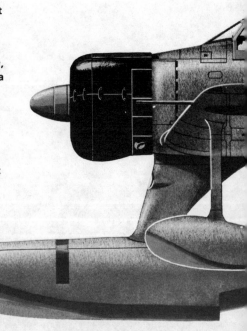

mishing had worn down his troops so much that only half of the 738 men were effective. To make matters worse only a small portion of the rations dropped from the air in that area had been recovered and the soldiers were hungry and their morale was low.

Liversedge decided to abandon the trail block but before ordering any movement he arranged for rations to be brought forward for the 3rd Battalion. After they had eaten, the blocking force was moved to Triri to rest and to prepare for the attack on Bairoko. While there the 3rd Battalion would send daily patrols down the Bairoko-Munda trail to obtain intelligence and to try and contact the Southern Landing Group which was supposed to be operating somewhere along that trail. At the same time patrols from the 1st Raider Regiment were reconnoitring the Enogai-Bairoko trail.

Colonel Currin and the 4th Raider Battalion arrived off Enogai at 0100 on 18th July and quickly unloaded five units of fire, fifteen days' rations and forty tons of supplies which they had brought with them. Liversedge now had the 1st and 4th Raider Battalions at Enogai and the army battalions holding Triri, and on 20th July the attack on Bairoko was launched. The army units were to attack from the inland trail leading to Bairoko and the Marines were to converge on it from the north crushing the Japanese between the two forces on the north east shore of Bairoko Harbour. At 0800 the army units left on the Bairoko trail and at 0830 the Marines, led by the 1st Raider Battalion, cleared Enogai. The army

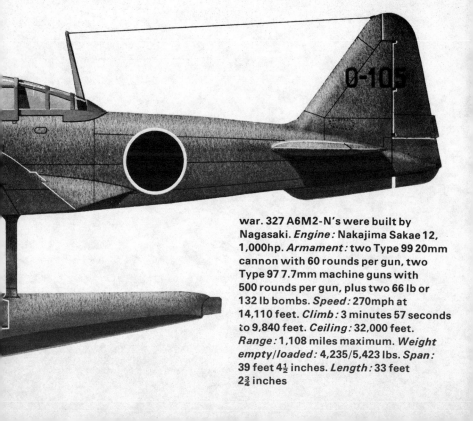

war. 327 A6M2-N's were built by Nagasaki. *Engine:* Nakajima Sakae 12, 1,000hp. *Armament:* two Type 99 20mm cannon with 60 rounds per gun, two Type 97 7.7mm machine guns with 500 rounds per gun, plus two 66 lb or 132 lb bombs. *Speed:* 270mph at 14,110 feet. *Climb:* 3 minutes 57 seconds to 9,840 feet. *Ceiling:* 32,000 feet. *Range:* 1,108 miles maximum. *Weight empty/loaded:* 4,235/5,423 lbs. *Span:* 39 feet 4½ inches. *Length:* 33 feet 2¾ inches

Jungle service for the dead

battalion under Lieutenant-Colonel Freer would protect the base at Triri and cover Rice Anchorage.

From 0955 when the first Japanese outpost was taken some 800 yards north east of the objective until late that evening, the attack by the army and Marines ran into very heavy fighting with a very determined enemy whose defences were so sited that they could not be reduced by the 60mm mortars of the Marines. The army units on the inland Bairoko trail likewise came up against positions so well prepared that they were stopped in their tracks and could make no move forward. Colonel Liversedge had asked for heavy air strikes on Bairoko harbour but they were not forthcoming and the Marines and army units suffered accordingly because they were too lightly armed to be able to dislodge the enemy who had spent many weeks preparing their positions and fought with fanatical

General Collins scans treetops over which mortar shells may pass

bravery.

At 1710 Lieutenant-Colonel Griffith returned to the regimental command post after touring all units and made a recommendation that the Marine force should retire. The casualty rate was such that there appeared to be more able bodied men carrying wounded than there were fighting and in fact over 200 of the force of less than 1,000 Marines were casualties and there were no reserves. Liversedge, having taken stock of the situation ordered his forces to withdraw to Enogai. This was done in an orderly fashion and just before dawn on 22nd July Colonel Liversedge sent the following message to be relayed to Guadalcanal: 'Request all available planes strike both sides Bairoko Harbour beginning 0900 You are covering our withdrawal.'

This message got through and must have had a powerful effect for Bairoko was bombed without ceasing from 0900 until dusk – over 130 tons of bombs being dropped in 250 sorties – the heaviest air strike of the campaign to date.

The wounded were evacuated by Catalina flying boats one of which was attacked by two Zero fighters and damaged so that it had to return to Enogai and spend the night under the shelter of the Marine Defence Battalion guns. The attack had failed and it had done so because the Marines and army units were too lightly armed for the operation and the vital air strikes had not materialised for no better reason than that the request arrived an hour later than the air coordination centre thought appropriate. However a substantial number of the Japanese had been prevented from reinforcing their hard pressed forces at Munda and it had caused General Sasaki to commit one reinforced battalion of the 13th Infantry, the greater portion of the Kure 6th SNLF and parts of the 7th SNLF, for the containment of the Allied Northern Landing Force. The fact that Admiral Turner's main objective was Munda and that he had not been given the additional resources for which he had asked in June made it obvious that he would have to concentrate on Munda to the detriment of the Bairoko attack. There had also been a wrong estimate of the enemy strength and capabilities in the Bairoko area based on lack of intelligence and the fact that the thick jungle and rain forest made aerial photographs practically valueless.

The Northern Landing Force now consolidated its position at Enogai and operated patrols from it to reconnoitre trails and enemy dispositions. It met occasionally with small Japanese patrols and the resulting clashes caused a few casualties on both sides but in general the situation remained static. On 3rd August the 3rd Battalion, 148th Infantry established a trail block on the Munda-Bairoko trail similar to the one they had set up originally, and two days later Liversedge, leading companies I and K, 145th Infantry regiment, Company D 1st Raider Battalion and a platoon of Company Q 4th Raiders, arrived at the trail block and relieved Lieutenant Schultz who then took his unit forward to Mount Tiariakiaba which dominated the main trails in the area but also overlooked Sunday Inlet.

On 9th August Colonel Liversedge, leading a composite patrol contacted a large patrol of American Infantry coming from the other direction. They were members of the 1st Battalion 27th Infantry, led by their commanding officer Lieutenant-Colonel Ryneska and this meeting completed the linking up of the Munda command and the Northern Landing Force. Next day the control of the Northern Landing Force passed into the operational control of the 25th Infantry Division and Major-General Collins placed the 1st Battalion 27th Infantry under Liversedge's command. Now the American forces began closing in on Bairoko. Slowly but inexorably the attack was pushed forward until finally, on 24th August, Bairoko was entered at 1700 without opposition. General Collins visited Enogai on 28th August and released the 1st Marine Raider Regiment. Next day the sadly depleted regiment embarked and returned to Guadalcanal.

Although Munda airfield fell on 5th August, and this date marked the end of the first phase of operation TOENAILS, there was much bitter fighting ahead and no one had any illusions about the fact that the Japanese were far from beaten. General Sasaki planned to hold a line on New Georgia from Bairoko Harbour to Sunday Inlet to the west and from this line he would launch his counterattack; but his plans depended on his having enough men and guns and for these he had looked to Admiral Kusaka who had earlier organised the runs of the 'Tokyo Express' by which fast Japanese destroyers had landed troops on Kolombangara Island with varying degrees of success. Indeed one such foray had led to the saga of PT 109, the Motor Torpedo Boat captained by Lieutenant John F Kennedy, later to become President of the United States.

109

PT 109

After the invasion of Rendova Island, the Motor Torpedo Boats and others of the same type had been stationed on and around the small islands of Kokorana and Lumbara inside Rendova Harbour which had been converted rapidly into bases capable of taking fifteen to twenty boats at any one time.

On 1st August an urgent Most Secret message was received by the Commanding Officer of the PT Base in Rendova Harbour from the Commander Task Force 31 on Guadalcanal, which indicated that the 'Tokio Express' was going to make an attempt to land men and supplies at Vila on Kolombangara Island that night. All the PT boats were sent out to intercept the enemy and Lieutenant Kennedy's boat, PT 109, was in Division B commanded by Lieutenant Henry J Brantingham in PT 159. The Division was ordered to cover the western part of Blackett Strait and the remaining boats were to block every other possible approach to Vila.

The north side of Kolombangara was to be covered by destroyers under command of Captain Burke together with another squadron of PT boats under Commander Kelly.

In Rabaul the Japanese command had decided to ferry 900 men and a large quantity of supplies to Kolombangara in three destroyers, the *Hagikaze*, the *Arashi* and the *Shigure*, with the destroyer *Amagiri* ('Heavenly Mist') as escort. By nightfall of the 1st August the four destroyers were clear of Bougainville Strait and steaming fast down 'the Slot' towards Vella Lavella on a course which would take them clear of Kundurumbangara point and then due south into Vella Gulf through Blackett Strait to land their troops and supplies at Vila on Kolombangara. The PT Boats soon located the approaching destroyers but there was poor communication between them and they did not inform each other of their intentions but attacked

PT boat at speed

110

individually. Their torpedo attacks were completely ineffective and at 0030 the *Hagikaze*, *Arashi* and *Shigure* were unloading at Vila with the *Amagiri* patrolling off shore. It took only forty-five minutes to unload their men and supplies and then the destroyers took up course and moved away at high speed. The night was extremely dark and, unknown to PT 109, she was directly in the path of the destroyer *Amagiri* which hit her without warning at thirty knots cutting the PT boat in two and immediately killing two of her crew. The stern sank at once leaving the bow floating and to this, after terrible exertions, the remaining members of the crew eventually made their way. Two of them, McMahon and Johnston, were so badly injured that they had to be rescued by Lieutenant Kennedy and Ensign Thom who swam with them pushing and pulling until they reached the ropes

hanging from the bow section.

The Coastwatcher on Kolombangara, Lieutenant R Evans, RANVR, had been watching that night and had seen a blaze and next morning, sweeping Blackett Strait with his binoculars he saw an object too far off to be identified, floating near the area in which he had seen the blaze. While reporting this he received a message from the Coastwatcher on Rendova telling him that PT 109 had been lost in action in Blackett Strait the night before. Lieutenant Evans immediately alerted his network of scouts and canoe patrols kept a sharp look out throughout the area.

As the day wore on the bow of PT 109 turned turtle and Lieutenant Ken-

Elco PT Boat. *Displacement:* 38 tons. *Length:* 80 feet. *Beam:* 20¾ feet. *Draught:* 5 feet. *Power/speed:* 3-shaft petrol engines, 4,050 shaft horse power/40 knots. *Armament:* four 21-inch torpedo tubes, or two torpedo tubes and eight depth charges, plus four .5-inch Browning machine guns and one 20mm cannon. *Crew:* fourteen

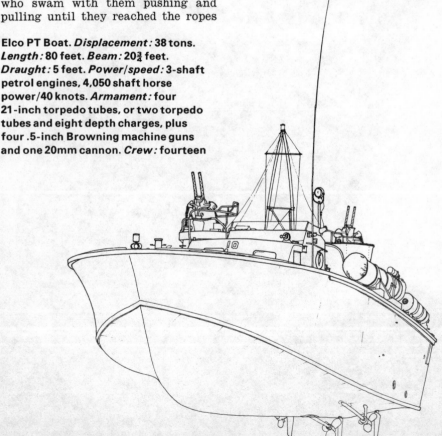

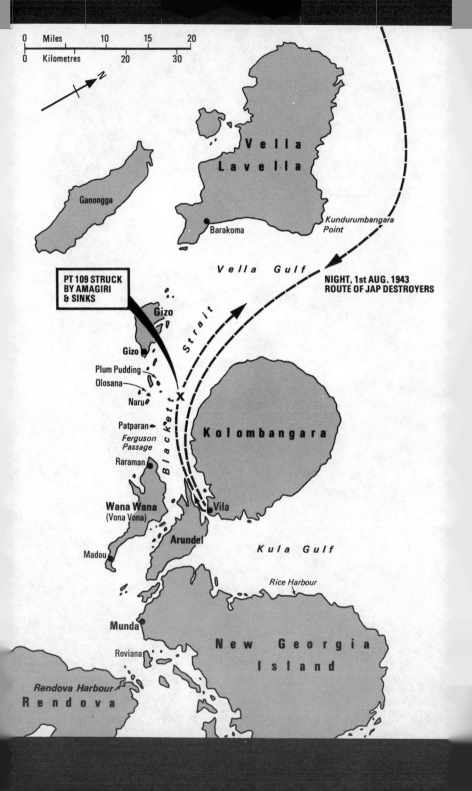

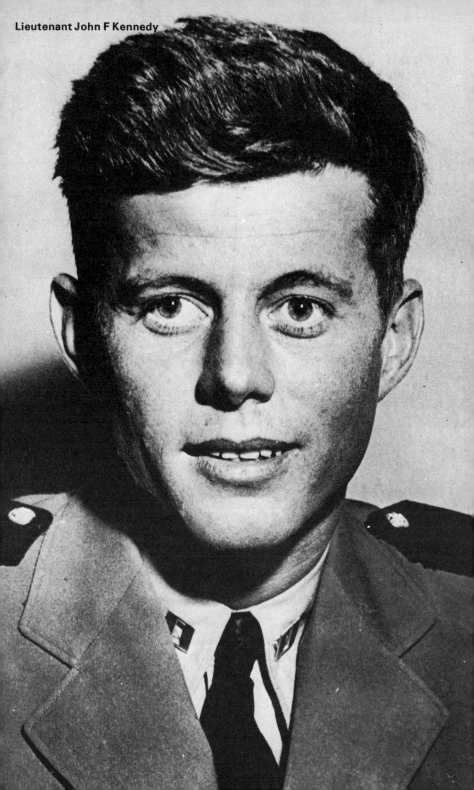

Lieutenant John F Kennedy

nedy decided that they must all swim to a small island called Plum Pudding which was one of a string of islets stretching south east from Gizo island. They put together a few planks and by dint of much swimming, pulling and pushing the wounded men, they all managed to reach the island. During the next two days and nights Lieutenant Kennedy and Ross swam out into Ferguson Passage to try to attract the attention of any PT boats which might be searching for them but without success. On the third day, in order to get coconuts for food and to get nearer to Ferguson passage, the group swam over to Olosana Island which is one and three quarter miles south west of Plum Pudding, and then, since Naru Island is only half a mile away and on the very edge of Ferguson passage Lieutenant Kennedy and Ross swam over to explore it, finding to their relief a canoe, rainwater and Japanese sweets in a wrapped bundle. They used the canoe to try to paddle to Rendova but

Floating dry-docks, Rendova base

kept falling out and had to give it up.

Not long after this two of Lieutenant Evans's scouts, Biuku Gasa and Eroni Kumana saw them but thought at first that they were Japanese and rapidly removed themselves, but at last Ensign Thom made them understand that the group were Americans by pointing to the sky and repeating the words 'White Star! White Star!' which all the islanders knew to be the insignia of the American aircraft – then Biuku and Eroni reacted favourably. On 6th August two messages, one carved by Lieutenant Kennedy on a coconut shell and the other written by Ross on an old invoice from Burns Philp Trading Company store at Gizo, were given to Biuku and Eroni to take to Rendova.

The two men paddled off to Raraman village in the Wana Wana lagoon and there met Ben Kevu, one of Lieutenant Evans's leading scouts. Ben sent a scout immediately to tell Lieutenant Evans what had happened while Biuku Eroni and another scout named John Kari from Madou village, set off for their night canoe trip to Rendova.

When Lieutenant Evans received the message it was past nightfall so very early next morning he sent off scouts Ben Kevu, Jonathan Bia, Joseph Eta, Stephen Hitu, Koete Igolo and Edward Kidoe in a large canoe to Lieutenant Kennedy at Naru Island with a letter in which he suggested that the leader of the party should return with the canoe so that they could work out full rescue operations for the rest of the survivors.

Meanwhile Biuku and his companions had reached the US Naval base on Roviana Island where they showed their messages. Immediately they were sent by PT boat to Rendova PT base which had already received a message from Lieutenant Kennedy through Lieutenant Evans and the Coastwatcher on Rendova. From then on events moved rapidly. The scouts had brought Lieutenant Kennedy over to Lieutenant Evans concealed under palm fronds in the bottom of the canoe – they had been buzzed by a Japanese plane in mid channel but had saved themselves and their passenger when Ben Kevu at the suggestion of

Jonathan Bia, stood up and waved to the plane which then went off. Shortly after 6pm the canoe had come ashore and Kennedy, scrambling out of his palm fronds, was greeted by Lieutenant Evans who took him to his hut for tea and a change of clothing. Such was Lieutenant Kennedy's weariness and excitement that later he was not able to remember Lieutenant Evans' name until sometime after he had been made President and then chance revealed that it was Lieutenant Evans and his scouts who had rescued him and his companions.

As soon as Kennedy had had some tea he and Evans composed a signal in which it was arranged for the PT boats to meet Lieutenant Kennedy in the canoe near Patparan Island and after that he would guide the PT boat to his crew. Soon after 8pm Kennedy said farewell to Evans and the scouts took him in their canoe to Patparan Island. For once everything went right and on Sunday 8th August, PT 157 took Kennedy and the survivors of his crew into Rendova Harbour one week after PT 109 had left her base.

Advance on the south coasts

Off the north west coast of New Georgia lie Arundel and Wana Wana Islands. They are both flat and featureless and covered with thick jungle and on their north side lies Kolombangara. Mangrove swamps grow round their shores and from the defence point of view the islands provide excellent ground over which to fight delaying actions especially if sufficient troops are available. General Sasaki had planned to retain a hold on the west coast of New Georgia and to use Arundel and Wana Wana islands as well but his plans were shattered by reason of a serious defeat suffered at sea.

On 6th August Admiral Kusaka ordered a task force of four destroyers to carry reinforcements from the Shortlands to Kolombangara Island. This method of increasing men and material in the forward fighting areas had been used successfully for some time despite Allied air and sea attacks and the troops and material, once landed on Kolombangara, would be deployed as required in the New Georgia area. On this occasion three destroyers were carrying 940 soldiers and 700 naval personnel and were jam packed while the fourth destroyer, acting as escort, had the normal ship's company aboard. The convoy arrived in Vella Gulf shortly before midnight and turned towards the Kolombangara beaches to unload. Admiral Wilkinson, who had taken over from Admiral Turner, had anticipated this attempt at reinforcement by the 'Tokyo Express' and task group 31.2 comprising destroyers *Dunlap, Craven, Maury, Lang, Sterrett* and *Stack* were carrying out a sweep along the west coast of Kolombangara under Commander F Moosbrugger USN. The task force was equipped with radar and as the Japanese approached they came up clearly on the screens of the US destroyers. Their attack took the Japanese completely by surprise and within a few minutes

4.2-inch mortar crew in action

torpedoes from the American destroyers had sunk the destroyer transports and the destroyer escort had turned tail and fled. None of the US destroyers was damaged.

This was the final Japanese attempt to reinforce General Sasaki and thereafter he had to make use of such troops and equipment as were immediately available to him. Sasaki now knew that he could not defeat the Allies and on 8-9th August he moved his headquarters to Kolombangara leaving the fighting on New Georgia, Arundel and Wana Wana islands to his subordinate commanders.

Griswold, being unaware at the time of Sasaki's plans, pushed ahead with his plans to trap the enemy on the west coast of New Georgia.

After the meeting between 1st Battalion 127th Infantry and the patrol led by Colonel Liversedge on the Bairoko-Munda trail, the 37th Division began to advance along the coast to the north under harassing small arms and artillery fire from the Japanese on Baanga and Arundel islands. A landing attempted by the Allies was repulsed and so, on the 10th August, the battle weary 43rd Division landed on Baanga to clear up the island. Meanwhile the 27th Infantry led by Colonel Sugg had swung southwards and wiped out the Japanese in the Zieta area killing 200, and by the 20th August, the 43rd Division, using four under strength battalions, had secured Baanga island, the few surviving Japanese escaping to Arundel and Kolombangara islands. Further to the north the 3rd Battalion, 148th Infantry, pushing south from Sunday Inlet met patrols of the 37th Division on the shores of Hathorn Sound but despite intense patrol activity nineteen barge loads of Japanese (composed largely of the 13th Infantry and the Kure 6th SNLF) withdrew

Left: 'Long Tom' on Rendova. *Below:* 'Pistol Pete' captured; one of two 5-inch Japanese naval guns on Baanga

from Bairoko Harbour to Kolombangara on the night of the 23rd, and after that date ground fighting on New Georgia ceased. However it was vital for General Sasaki to hold out as long as he could (Japanese Imperial Headquarters Navy Staff Directive No. 267 dated 13th August 1943) to permit Admiral Kusaka and General Imamura to strengthen defences in the northern Solomons, the intention being that in late September or early October the entire Japanese force would be withdrawn from the Central Solomons.

The range and hitting power of the Marine 155mm guns made them ideal weapons for bombarding Kolombangara from the shores of Hathorn Sound and preliminary reconnaissance showed that the best site for them would be on Piru plantation just north and to the east of Diamond Narrows. The guns and their ancillary equipment were unloaded on 30th August in full view of the enemy 12,000 yards away on Kolombangara. As a result when the first shells from the Marine 'Long Toms' landed on Japanese positions in and around the Vila airstrip, it was only a few minutes before the Japanese gunners retaliated and shells fell near the Marine gun positions which however, suffered no damage as they were in defilade behind hills.

This artillery duel continued throughout the following days on a basis which was more or less personal. At night a seaplane based on Vila on Kolombangara would circle the Marine guns positions and drop small bombs which did no damage but robbed the men of their sleep and annoyed them intensely.

These were followed by a few rounds of shell fire which further exacerbated the men. During the day the Japanese would fire at the American positions at their meal times (which resulted in lost food and the further ruffling of tempers) and they also had the habit of shelling boats landing near the best observation post (a tall tree near the beach from which the fall of shot on Kolombangara could be observed). The Marines retaliated by firing at the Japanese gun flashes and the enemy tried to trick them by setting off powder flashes distant from the actual gun sites at the moment of firing but these ruses were soon found out when the Marines realised that there was a discrepancy between the number of flashes and the number of shot falling in their area.

The Marines then put up a spotter plane which was so effective (despite heavy anti-aircraft fire) that the Japanese gun positions were shelled with extreme accuracy and thereafter went out of action or were unwilling to continue the duel. In order to retaliate for the shelling at meal times, the Marines made careful note of the smoke from cooking fires and put down shell bursts on or very near them and this further discouraged the enemy. Initially the anti-aircraft fire from Kolombangara was too accurate for the Allies and resulted in the loss of nine spotter aircraft. Thereupon a plan was devised with the help of COMAIRSOLS whereby specific positions were heavily shelled and then, at a pre-determined time, dive bombers would appear and attack the enemy anti-aircraft positions which in theory would have been deserted by their crews, but very soon the Japanese caught on to the American plan and they would leave their anti-aircraft posts as soon as the Marine 155mm guns began to fire and return as soon as they had stopped to man their anti-aircraft guns and fire at the attacking dive bombers. The Marines then went one further. They fired as before and the enemy, taking the hint, would disperse only to return when the Marine fire stopped and the dive bombers appeared – but the dive bombers did not attack – instead they remained high – and the Marine gunners then poured in more shells catching the Japanese in their open emplacements. After several of these co-ordinated attacks the pilots of the dive bombers reported that the anti-

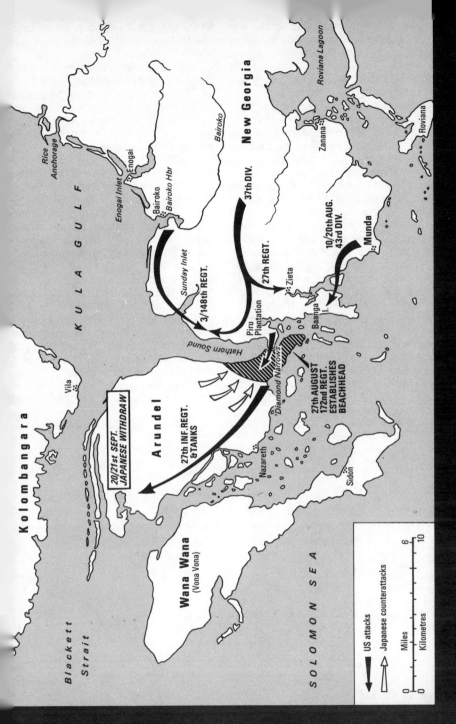

Clearing New Georgia and Arundel

aircraft fire was most ineffective and had dwindled almost to nothing. Later, in mid October, a battalion of the 25th Infantry Division going ashore found that the Japanese guns, emplacements and camp sites had been thoroughly smashed up by the shelling and bombing.

The move of Allied forces in the shape of the 172nd Infantry, to Arundel island, was carried out unopposed on 27th August. In a sense this was unfortunate as it gave the impression that the enemy had removed themselves leaving only a few snipers to harass the Americans. A beachhead was quickly established but before the Americans had started to sweep the island, General Sasaki attacked with units of his 13th Infantry which struck the 172nd from different points at varying times tying them down and causing so much havoc that reinforcements had to be sent in, but even with these the 172nd found it difficult to contain a well planned and desperate Japanese attack on the morning of 15th September. The Allied drive came to a standstill and

the Japanese, with far fewer troops committed could claim a moral victory.

As a result General Griswold ordered Colonel Sugg to take the 27th Infantry and the Marine Tank units to Arundel, assume overall command and drive out the enemy. On the night of 16th and 17th September, under cover of heavy rain, Colonel Sugg moved the tanks and a battalion of infantry over to Arundel and at first light the next morning five tanks from 11th Defence Battalion closely supported by Company C, 27th Infantry, attacked a particularly vicious enemy strongpoint and taking it by surprise overran the position. The enemy counterattacked immediately and for a time the American infantry could not follow the tanks, but the sudden tank attack had disorganised the Japanese and they had no reserves to follow up their counterattack and soon the Allies had moved forward 500 yards and consolidated their position without loss of a single tank.

The initial success of the tanks had convinced Sugg that they could

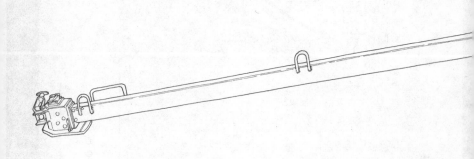

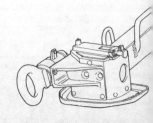

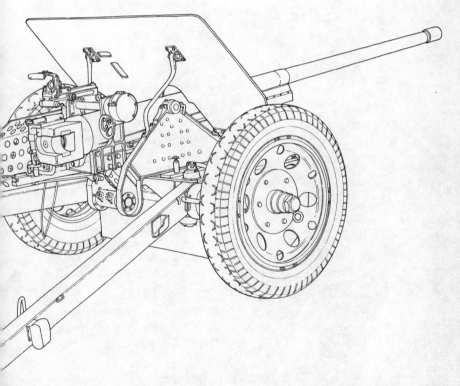

The Japanese Model 1 (1941) 47mm anti-tank gun. *Calibre:* 47mm. *Weight:* 1,600 lbs. *Muzzle velocity:* 2,735 feet per second. *Range:* 8,400 yards. *Traverse:* 60 degrees. *Elevation:* −11 degrees to +19 degrees. *Ammunition:* AP and HE (3.37 lbs in weight). *Penetration:* 1½ inches of homogenous steel plate at 20 degrees at 1,400 yards

Serving a 155mm howitzer

Emergency operations are performed in the field

Engineers transport infantry across a river

repeat the performance, and on 18th September a four tank attack was sent forward supported once again by infantry but during the night the enemy had hidden two 37mm anti-tank guns in the thick forest and these, coming into action, knocked out two tanks before they had advanced fifty yards. However, the accompanying infantry put down a very heavy concentration of small arms fire from automatic weapons and rifles and enabled the crews of the crippled tanks to escape unharmed. Next morning eleven tanks with infantry support went back to attack and this time a combination of gun-fire from the tanks and close support

40mm gun crew on the alert, Munda

from the infantry, who prevented the Japanese from planting magnetic mines on the tanks and also kept Japanese anti-tank gunners away from their guns, resulted in success. On the night of 20th-21st September, the Japanese withdrew from Arundel island leaving only a few stragglers who either died fighting or saved themselves by swimming across to Kolombangara.

Munda airstrip was now secure from harassment by artillery fire and could only be attacked from the sea (an unlikely event as the Allied task forces provided continuous protection in the area) or from the air. In the fighting for New Georgia General Sasaki lost 345 dead and some 500 of his men were wounded but he had

carried out his orders for he had delayed the Allied advance and had saved the greater part of his forces to withdraw from the Central Solomons leaving 44 Americans dead and 256 wounded.

The original intention had been to push the Japanese out of Kolombangara as a prelude to attacks on Japanese positions to the north but on reflection Admiral Halsey came to the conclusion that it would be much more profitable to by-pass the heavily defended Kolombangara, immobilising it from sea and air, and to seize the lightly held island of Vella Lavella fourteen miles to the north west. The advantages of this move were that it would provide a forward marine and air base for operations against the enemy further north; it would also provide a means of cutting across the enemy supply line and in theory should compel the enemy on Kolombangara to withdraw or starve. The added attraction was that Lieutenants Josselyn and Firth, RANVR, the Coastwatchers on Vella Lavella, had the island very well organised and the islanders, as in other parts of the Solomons, were under administrative control although the Japanese were quite unaware of this. (Lieutenant Josselyn was a District Officer in the British Solomon Islands administration as well as being a Coastwatcher.) The Allies could therefore expect one hundred per cent cooperation and assistance in all phases of the landing and subsequent fighting.

Breakthrough to Vella Lavella

Admiral Halsey's proposals were agreed and during the night of 21st and 22nd July, long before the fighting on Arundel had finished, a six man patrol of Army, Navy and Marine officers landed near the south-east tip of Vella Lavella close to Barakoma village. At the time there were about 600 Japanese manning various posts round the coasts of Vella Lavella and an additional 500 who had managed to get ashore from barges which had been sunk. The patrol was met by Lieutenant Josselyn and under his guidance and that of his scouts they spent a week scouting the island thoroughly. The information they gathered was full and precise and on their return to Guadalcanal on 31st July, the patrol was able to report that a landing in the vicinity of Barakoma was perfectly feasible.

Admiral Halsey decided that the landing and occupation force, which was to be 6,505 strong, was to be called the Northern Landing Force and was to be under command of Major-General R B McClure, assistant commander of the 25th Division. McClure would have in his command the 35th Regimental Combat Team US Army, the 58th Naval Construction Battalion, the Marine 4th Defence Battalion to provide anti-aircraft and sea defences, the 25th Cavalry Reconnaissance Troops and other army and naval detachments.

Prior to the landing Lieutenant-Commander Mackenzie, RAN, commanding the Coastwatchers from Guadalcanal, had foreseen the need for extra staff on the Coastwatchers' base on Vella Lavella and arrangements were made to send forward Writer J Mungovern, RAN, and Corporal Cunningham, US Army, so that Lieutenants Josselyn and Firth would be freer to move about with the Allied forces. Owing to the large number of Japanese on the island it was no longer possible to use Catalina flying boats to bring in and take out Allied

USS Selfridge after Vella Lavella

LCT (4) *Displacement:* 611 tons. *Length:* 187¼ feet. *Beam:* 38¾ feet. *Draught:* 3¾/4½ feet. *Power/speed:* 2-shaft Davey Paxman diesel engines, 920 hp/10 knots. *Armament:* two 20mm cannon. *Load:* six 40-ton tanks, or nine 30-ton tanks, or twelve 3-ton lorries, or 300 tons of cargo. *Crew:* twelve

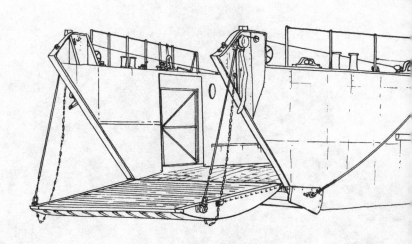

The shelling of Vila airfield on Kolombangara

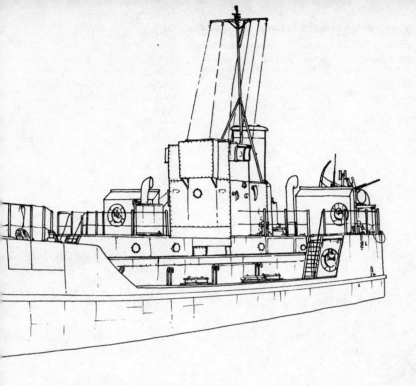

Attacks on Guadalcanal continue – a raider flees from AA fire

Japanese bombing attack on shipping at Guadalcanal

troops – instead motor torpedo boats were used to land them by night and take out any rescued personnel or units whose missions had been completed, and Mungovern and Cunningham were put into Vella Lavella in this manner.

One most unfortunate aspect of the preparations to move forward into Vella Lavella was the bombing and strafing of friendly villages by Allied pilots who were unfamilar with the area. All the Coastwatchers suffered from this and there were strong protests from Josselyn and Firth on Vella Lavella, Waddell and Seton on Choiseul and Evans on Kolombangara, for it was essential to retain the goodwill of the people and it was made very clear to the Allied headquarters that unless the pilots were very much more careful, there was a grave risk not only of alienating loyal islanders but also of drying up the sources of Intelligence on which the Coastwatchers, and through them the Allies, relied so much. Thereafter pilots on missions taking them over unfamiliar ground were required first to fly reconnaissance and only then to set out on their bombing missions, and this did much to check indiscriminate bombing and strafing.

Embarkation of the Task Force began during the morning of 12th August at Guadalcanal and on that night a twenty-five-man Army-Marine team left from Rendova and went ashore at Barakoma to mark the beaches for the use of landing craft on DDay. It was decided to reinforce this unit on 14th August by an army infantry company in case there was need to defend them against the numbers of Japanese armed with small arms who were moving about the island. In the event there was no contact and the Japanese remained unaware that there were Allied forces on the island let alone that the Coastwatchers and their scouts had been there for over a year. The night of 14th August was cloudless and there was a brilliant moon when the task force sailed for Vella Lavella. There were attacks by enemy planes on Guadalcanal, New Georgia and the Russells that night but apparently the convoy was not seen for it arrived off Barakoma at 0600 next morning untouched, and Allied aircraft from Munda airfield arrived overhead at the same time to mount a covering patrol. It was very seldom during the Solomons campaign that a landing worked without any hitches and the unloading and beachhead establishment at Barakoma was no exception. The pre-operational patrol reports and photographic reconnaissance had failed to disclose a submerged coral reef twenty yards offshore from the beach where the 2nd Battalion, 35th Infantry were to make the first landing and as a result the LCIs carrying the unit grounded offshore with a stretch of deep water between them and the beach.

Colonel Brown, in command of the 1st Battalion therefore went directly in to the beach assigned to him and made the initial landing while the 2nd Battalion, having backed off the reef, came in to the north on the 1st Battalion beach. This led to congestion and confusion and that, plus wrongly interpreted visual messages, resulted in further delay so that the unloading from the LCTs was not completed until 0900. This was not the end of the difficulties, for the larger LSTs following the LCIs beached in relatively deep water making it impossible to unload. The situation was saved by a Lieutenant of the Naval Construction Battalion who used a bulldozer to scrape up coral ramps from the beaches to the bow doors and although unloading went on apace all day the LSTs departed at 1800 with some of the 4th Defence Battalion gear still on board.

At 0759 the Japanese made their first attack on the beachhead and the shipping offshore using six bombers and eleven fighters and causing some damage. The next attack came at approximately 0900 when fourteen enemy aircraft evaded the Allied

General McClure

Loading fuel at a jungle dump

Major-General Barrowclough

NZ troops relieve US units, Baka Baka beach, Vella Lavella

Wreckage at Vila airstrip, Kolombangara Island

planes patrolling overhead and again caused some damage. This attack was followed at noon by eleven bombers and forty-eight fighters and it found the LCIs leaving the beachhead. The final attack of the day came at 1730 just before the LSTs were ready to leave, when eight bombers and forty-five fighters made an attack. Despite these attacks during which the Japanese lost seventeen planes and the Americans had twelve men killed and forty wounded, General McClure had ashore 4,600 troops and 3,200 tons of supplies of all classes by nightfall. This gave him enough to support his force for fifteen days. In addition the beach defences had been set up and the Naval Construction Battalions (the SEABEES) had begun work to clear the jungle along the shore in preparation for the construction of an airstrip.

On the night of 15th August, Admiral Kusaka conferred with General Imamura and suggested that a battalion of Japanese infantry be sent to Vella Lavella with the intention of attacking the Allied Task Force. General Imamura, however, was a realist and pointed out that to send a battalion against the large number of men brought ashore by General McClure would be a waste of men and there was also the fact (unknown at the time to General McClure) that Imperial Headquarters in Tokyo had ordered that Japanese forces in the Central Solomons should fall back slowly reducing the Allied strength as much as possible with the intention, finally, of defending Rabaul to the last man. It was for this reason that General McClure faced no serious opposition during the seizure of the beachhead on Vella Lavella.

Outside the perimeter surrounding the beachhead the Japanese held posts on the north east coast and their barge traffic still went on. The Coastwatchers reported that there was a movement of

Seashore airfield at Vella Lavella; fighters await mission

enemy troops in large parties across the island towards the north coast and it was decided that they should be forced into a pocket on the north-west peninsula of the island and there destroyed. For this task General Mc-Clure decided to use the 3rd New Zealand Division commanded by Major-General Barrowclough. On the 18th September this Division landed at Barakoma to relieve the 35th Infantry. The New Zealand Division brought with them the South Pacific Scouts who were invaluable in reconnaissance and ambush and proved to be the eyes and ears of many patrol actions during the following weeks. On 21st September the New Zealand Division began a two pronged drive to force the enemy into the north west corner of the island. The Japanese, under orders to delay the Allies as long as possible, fought stubbornly and it was not until the 5th and 6th October that the enemy were pocketed and the concentrated fire of mortars, machine guns and two field batteries began to register in the area.

During the fighting on Vella Lavella the Japanese had been moving their troops from Kolombangara to the island of Choiseul and by the beginning of October there were no Japanese units of any size left on Kolombangara. There was no need, therefore, to maintain an outpost on Vella Lavella and at midnight on 6th October, a Japanese convoy consisting of nine destroyers, five submarine chasers and three motor torpedo boats sailed from Rabaul and Kieta on Bougainville island, to evacuate the Japanese remaining on Vella Lavella. As they were approaching land the convoy was contacted by an American group of three destroyers under Captain F B Walker and in the ensuing battle the Japanese lost the destroyer *Yugumo* and the Americans lost the *Chevalier*, but this did not prevent the Japanese from evacuating their men so that the final assault by the 3rd New Zealand Division on the north west pocket met with very little opposition.

The Allies move north

Admiral Halsey had decided, some time before the fighting on the island had ceased, to establish a forward operating base on Vella Lavella, and on 17th September the Commanding General 1st Marine Amphibious Corps, Major-General C D Barrett, was ordered to take the necessary action. The task force created for this purpose was under the command of Major D M Schmuck and was created from units of the 77th Naval Construction Battalion, 3rd Special Weapons Battalion, the Motor Transport Corps, 4th Base Depot, a communications group from the 3rd Amphibious Force and specially detailed officers and men from the 3rd Marine Division.

Such a mixed force inevitably required shakedown training and when this had been put in hand orders were issued for the operation to take place on 23rd September. There was to be a landing near Ruravai on the east coast and a landing further south on the same coast at the Juno river. One assault unit in two APDs (Assault Purpose Destroyers) would land near Ruravai and the other unit in one APD would land near the mouth of the Juno River. One hour after each landing supporting LSTs would beach at each landing point bringing in additional troops, supplies and heavy equipment. The landings were to be protected from the air and the sea and after the landings the two units would link up at Ruravai where the projected base was to be constructed.

The small convoy set sail from Guadalcanal at noon on 23rd September, and having carried out a practice landing at Tetere it sailed north without interference through a calm sea. However, late reconnaissance reports received early on the morning of 25th September led to a change of plans. It appeared that the beaches at Ruravai, which it had been intended to use, were unsuitable for the landing craft (Higgins boats, said to be constructed on the lines of boats used by

Supplies build-up on Rendova

142

Admiral Halsey with backdrop of Old Glory

Major-General Barrett, USMC

rum runners during prohibition days in the United States) and therefore all unloading would have to be done at Juno beach. Major Schmuck changed his plans an hour before the landing but for once the messages got through to the right quarters and there were no serious hitches when landing began at 0700 on schedule. At 0720 all assault troops were ashore and the cargoes on the APDs unloaded whereupon Major Schmuck handed over command of the Juno area to his executive officer Captain R E Patterson and taking one company, set off along the coast for Ruravai to establish a beachhead for the LST due to arrive there.

The beachhead was secured and by 1115 the LST was unloaded and the cargo was well dispersed with the destroyers screening the operation hull down on the horizon. Suddenly fifteen enemy dive bombers escorted by fighters began to attack the destroyers and then to attack the beachhead as well, coming in from the direction of the sun making it very difficult for the anti-aircraft gunners to find their targets. LST 167 was hit and despite heavy fire which knocked down at least four enemy aircraft, there was heavy damage to the supplies and installations on the beach. Thirty-two of the Americans were killed and the fifty-eight wounded were taken by small boat to the New Zealand field hospital further down the coast to the south. The fact that there were not more casualties was a tribute to the use of fox holes which had been dug as soon as the troops had gone ashore.

In this particular instance Major Schmuck was without radar or an early warning system of air attack, and to afford more protection the number of anti-aircraft guns was increased by the addition of Battery A 70th Coast Artillery, which had 90mm anti-aircraft guns and radar. This battery was in position and in action on 28th September in Narowai plantation between Ruravai and Juno. The next serious enemy air raid occurred

at 0930 on 1st October. LSTs were unloading the 2nd Parachute Battalion, Fleet Marine Force, together with other units, when a large formation of enemy fighters and dive bombers attacked them. LST 448 was hit and set on fire and there were many casualties in the dispersal areas and amongst the defences but, as a slight recompense, one Japanese plane was shot down. At 1000 on the same morning the Japanese attacked again and this time LST 334 was hit while still on the beach at Ruravai. At 1435 the enemy struck again with sixty planes but the Allied air patrol was on station at the time and only a few bombers penetrated the fighter screen to hit LST 448 once again. The final attack of the day at 1900 destroyed five heavy trucks and three jeeps. Following these raids and the losses they caused it was decided that all resupply ships for Vella Lavella should unload at Barakoma where there were much heavier anti-aircraft defences manned by the 4th Marine Defence Battalion, and the material required by Major Schmuck could then be carried north along the shore by truck. The enemy, however, kept well clear of Barakoma and struck only at Ruravai on 3rd and 6th October where wide dispersal of troops and supplies together with an allied air patrol, and the heavy anti-aircraft fire of the 90mm battery, kept casualties down to a minimum. By 8th October the Corps Staging Area was considered secure and the Forward Echelon created for the purpose was dissolved. In its short life it had lost 149 men in dead, wounded and missing.

The Japanese had built airfields on Mono island and on Ballali island in the Shortlands group which lies just south east of Bougainville and constitutes the beginning of the British Solomon Islands Protectorate as distinguished from the islands of the northern Solomons such as Bougainville, Buka etc, which are administered under an Australian mandate. These airfields and the Japanese garrisons

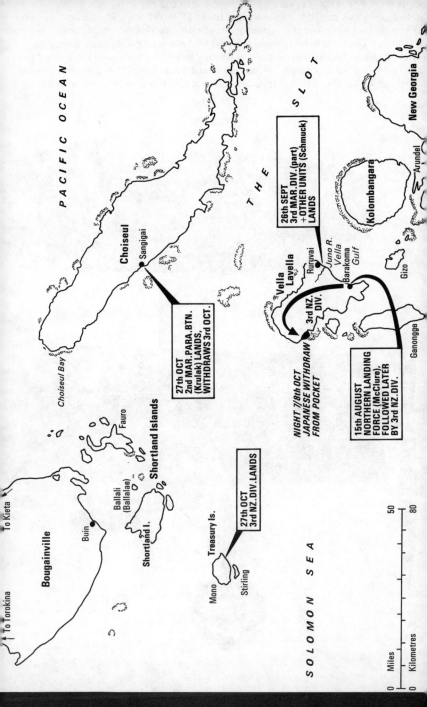

PACIFIC OCEAN

Choiseul

Sangigai

Choiseul Bay

THE SLOT

New Georgia

Arundel

Kolombangara

Gizo

Vella Lavella

Ruruvai

Juno R.

Vella Gulf

Barakoma

Ganongga

26th SEPT
3rd MAR.DIV. (part)
+ OTHER UNITS (Schmuck)
LANDS

27th OCT
2nd MAR.PARA.BTN.
(Krulak) LANDS,
WITHDRAWS 3rd OCT.

3rd N.Z.
DIV.

NIGHT 7/8th OCT
JAPANESE WITHDRAW
FROM POCKET

15th AUGUST
NORTHERN LANDING
FORCE (McClure),
FOLLOWED LATER
BY 3rd N.Z. DIV.

Shortland Islands

Fauro

Ballali
(Ballalae)

Shortland I.

Buin

Bougainville

To Kieta

To Torokina

Treasury Is.

27th OCT
3rd N.Z.DIV. LANDS

Mono

Stirling

SOLOMON SEA

Miles   50

Kilometres   80

To Vella Lavella and the Treasury Islands

The Grumman F6F-3 Hellcat was a development of the F6F-1 fighter which Grumman were designing as a possible replacement for the F4F Wildcat. The design was still in its infancy at the time of the Japanese attack on Pearl Harbor, and soon Grumman were able to incorporate the lessons learned by American pilots in combat into their new fighter. This comprised more armour and armament, and confirmed the need for self-sealing fuel tanks. When it reached operational theatres, the Hellcat proved to be superior in most respects to almost all Japanese fighters; it was

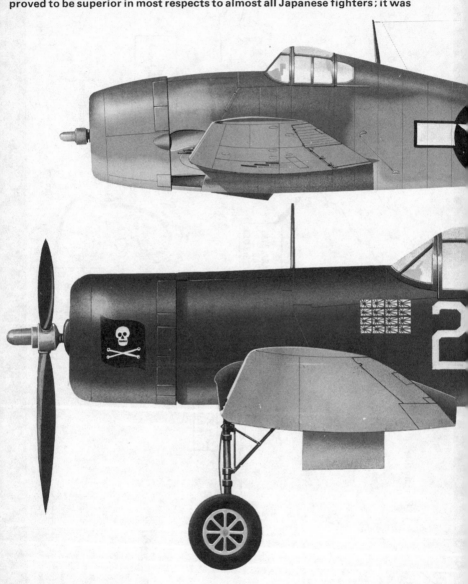

faster, stronger, better protected, more heavily armed, possessing a better climbing and diving speed, and was also extremely manoeuvrable for its size and loaded weight. *Engine:* Pratt &Whitney R-2800 radial, 2,000hp. *Armament:* six .5-inch Browning machine guns with 400 rounds per gun. *Speed:* 376mph at 17,300 feet. *Climb:* 3,500 feet per minute initially. *Ceiling:* 38,400 feet. *Range:* 1,090 miles on internal fuel. *Weights empty/loaded:* 9,042/11,381 pounds. *Span:* 42 feet 10 inches. *Length:* 33 feet 7 inches

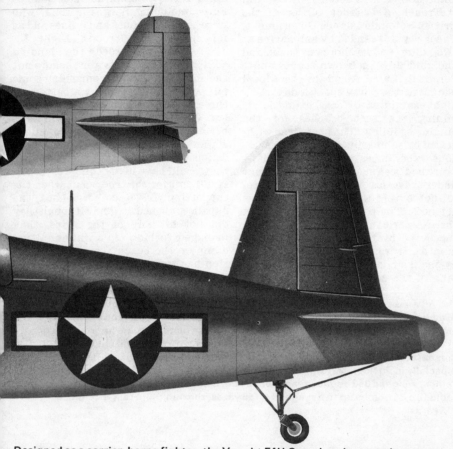

Designed as a carrier-borne fighter, the Vought F4U Corsair only started to operate from carriers in the summer of 1944, as the type had previously been considered not suitable for this operational use, despite the fact that the Fleet Air Arm had been using it from carriers since the summer of 1943. The first US squadrons to use the Corsair operationally were the land-based units of the US Marine Corps. The type proved equally successful in the fighter and fighter-bomber roles, and by the end of the war had destroyed 2,140 Japanese aircraft for a loss of only 189 Corsairs. The F4U possessed a very good turn of speed, and could thus offer or decline combat as it wished against slower Japanese machines. *Engine:* Pratt &Whitney R-2800 radial, 2,250hp. *Armament:* six .5-inch Browning machine guns with 400 rounds per gun, plus two 1,000 pound bombs or eight 5-inch rockets. *Speed:* 425mph at 20,000 feet. *Climb rate:* 3,120 feet per minute initially. *Ceiling:* 37,000 feet. *Range:* 1,015 miles on internal fuel. *Weight empty/loaded:* 8,694/13,120 pounds. *Span:* 40 feet 11 inches *Length:* 33 feet 4 inches

stationed thereon had to be captured and the task was given to the 3rd New Zealand Division which had by now consolidated its hold on Vella Lavella.

Early reconnaissance of Mono island was undertaken by a party of Marines and Solomon islanders led by Captain D Trench, a District Officer of the British Solomon Islands Government. The party was landed by submarine at two points on the shores of the island and guided by their own scouts under Sergeant Ilala. Aided by the local islanders, the party spent a day and a night examining all features and determining the best beaches for the landing to follow. The party was withdrawn by submarine after some hazardous experiences but the reconnaissance had been successfully carried out under the noses of the enemy and careful notes were taken of the Japanese defences. The party also brought out three American airmen who had been succoured by the islanders for some months. It was this kind of aid given by the islanders from the very beginning of the campaign which made it

virtually certain that the Japanese in the Solomons were fighting a losing battle.

The New Zealand Division landed on Mono island at the end of October taking with them Captain Bentley and units of the Solomon Islands Defence Force including Sergeant Ilala, who were to act as scouts and guides and as forward guerilla troops. Eight US destroyers bombarded the landing area before the troops went ashore but the shelling, although smashing some pill boxes did not destroy a battery of three five-pounder mountain guns and two 3-inch mortars overlooking the beach. These guns remained silent while the landing was proceeding which was extremely fortunate since they could have made things extremely difficult for the troops but when the supporting LSTs came ashore the Japanese opened fire and although they did not hit any of the ships, they managed to blow up an ammunition dump on the beach. The enemy position had to be destroyed and the New Zealand unit detailed to carry out the

The Japanese Model 94 (1934) 90mm mortar was a smooth bore, muzzle loading and fixed firing-pin weapon, unusual among mortars in having two recoil cylinders, mounted on a U-shaped frame attached to the base plate. A much improved version of the Model 94 was the Model 97, which did away with the recoil mechanism, and thus saved 120 pounds in weight, making the weapon much easier to handle, especially in difficult terrain. The type was capable of firing HE and incendiary bombs, weighed 340 pounds ready for action, measured 51 inches in length and could fire its bombs up to a range of 4,155 yards, the minimum range being 612 yards

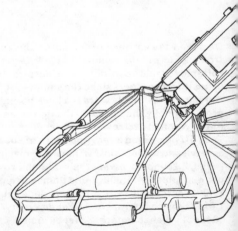

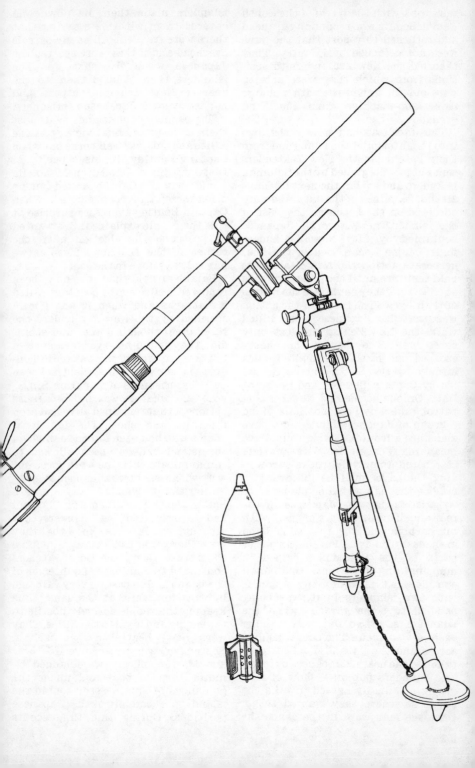

task took with them two of the South Pacific Scouts who reconnoitred ahead and returned to report that the guns were not defended by infantry. They then led the New Zealanders to positions from which they were able to wipe out the gun crews with a charge using sub-machine guns and hand grenades.

The Japanese had now withdrawn into the interior of the island and from their beachhead the New Zealanders sent out patrols guided by the Solomon islanders and within the next few days all that remained of the Japanese were cornered on the beach on the west of the island. There were 175 Japanese contained by fifty New Zealanders under Major Logan, and in the final desperate action the New Zealanders held their fire until the Japanese were so close that they could 'see the whites of their eyes'. The result of the action was that 120 Japanese were killed while the New Zealanders lost only three men. The rest of the enemy escaped and later were hunted down largely by the South Pacific Scouts led by Captain Bentley and Sergeant Ilala. On one occasion a New Zealand patrol guided by Sergeant Ilala found a group of Japanese hidden in a cave and since a frontal attack would have meant many casulaties, Sergeant Ilala clambered among the rocks surrounding the cave until he discovered a crevice through which he managed to wriggle, taking the Japanese in the rear and disposing of six of them with his carbine and the rest with hand grenades. The islanders, as in other parts of the Solomons, helped in mopping up operations. One small episode was typical of many. A canoe, with two islanders in it, was being paddled to some gardens when the islanders saw two Japanese waving excitedly to them. The canoe paddled across and the Japanese asked to be taken to the nearest Japanese outpost. The islanders put on a show of misgiving but finally agreed to take the Japanese where they wanted to go. Once the men were in the canoe the

islanders made them lie down and covered them with mats saying that there were frequent Allied air patrols overhead and if they were spotted the Japanese would be shot up. The islanders then paddled them to the nearest New Zealand outpost and handed over the Japanese as prisoners.

The people of the islands never lost their faith in the final victory of the Allies and this was well borne out when Captain Bentley, in his capacity of District Officer, landed on Mono. He found that the Chief had died but no other chief had been elected. When Captain Bentley expressed surprise at this the people explained: 'We wanted to postpone the election until the return of the District Officer as we have always done in the past'

Balali airfield had by now been rendered ineffective by constant Allied air attacks and when it was finally stormed by the New Zealanders the resistance, though fierce, was sporadic. They found however, evidence of the way in which the Japanese conducted their war. The airfield had been built by prisoners of war from Singapore and when it was finished those prisoners that remained alive had been lined up and shot. The few local people who had been forced to work on the island had not been allowed to communicate with the work force but were witnesses of what happened.

Lieutenant Waddell and Captain Seton, the Coastwatchers on Choiseul had so organised the islanders that although the Japanese knew that they were there, and had sent a large force to capture them, the Coastwatchers continued to dominate the interior of the island and to pass on very valuable information while at the same time keeping the people actively hostile to the enemy and loyal to the Allies. They were greatly heartened when, early in September, a patrol of five US Navy and Marine officers were landed by motor torpedo boat and under the guidance of Captain Seton toured the island to reconnoitre the Japanese positions. During this time scouts carrying messages travelled thirty-five miles through the jungle in the dark in nine hours – a remarkable feat and again indicative of the trust and courage of the islanders. The combined patrol, on its return to base, reported favourably and later in September a second patrol of nine was landed to examine the north west of the island. On the day they left after having been guided by Captain Seton, another patrol of ten men was landed to carry out an examination of the southern end of the island.

Again Captain Seton guided this party and when they had been shown everything by moving around and through the Japanese in the area, they were taken out by torpedo boat together with several pilots who had been picked up by Coastwatchers and looked after for some weeks.

The original intention had been to land sufficient forces on the island to wipe out the four thousand or more Japanese who were estimated to be in camp or moving about on Choiseul. However the plans were changed and instead the policy of 'island hopping' was instituted which meant that Choiseul was to be by-passed, as also was Buin, and Torokina on Bougainville was to be occupied. This occupation would provide a fighter strip within range of Rabaul and so provide cover for the bombers during their frequent raids. To provide a diversion from the main operation there was to be a raid on the Japanese posts around the centre and the north west of the island carried out by Marine paratroops who were to be landed from barges.

Towards the end of October Seton was brought out by motor torpedo boat together with scouts who knew the areas to be attacked and together he and his men briefed the Marine Paratroops who were then on Vella Lavella. Lieutenant Waddell, who remained on Choiseul, carried on with his Coastwatching duties and at the same time made arrangements for the

US Troops inspect hidden Japanese dugouts in the jungle

reception of the raiding party and mustered carriers at the proposed landing point. On the night of 27th October Lance-Corporal Pitakere piloted the first landing craft in to the large village of Sangigai to be met by Lieutenant Waddell, and soon the Parachute Battalion with its supplies and equipment was hidden in the jungle. During the next two days the paratroops prepared a camp with defensive positions while Seton took Colonel Krulak, the commanding officer of the Parachute Battalion, to reconnoitre the Japanese positions.

Colonel Krulak decided to wipe out the Japanese near Sangigai and planned to do this by sending one party under Captain Stafford to attack them from the front while he led another party to attack them from the rear. Accordingly before dawn on 31st October, landing barges took Captain Stafford and his party along the shore to a beach already scouted and known

Further Solomons landings en route to Bougainville

to be clear of the enemy. The coastal party drove in from the beach and after some fierce fighting the Japanese retreated and ran into Colonel Krulak's party who had reached their objective and had turned towards the beach. Captain Seton and his scouts were leading the Paratroops up a hill when the first contacts were made. In the first burst of fire five Japanese were killed. The enemy then withdrew, reformed and charged madly down the hill firing as they came. The Paratroops held their fire until the enemy were close then mowed them down with heavy and accurate bursts from automatic weapons followed by a bayonet charge. A large number of Japanese were killed but an enemy machine gun on the left flank continued to harass the men until a patrol sent out to deal with it killed the Japanese manning it. Captain Seton had arranged a very suitable area for the Paratroops to bivouac that night but the Colonel ordered all troops to return to the beach for embarkation in the barges and return to base camp.

The two units reached the beach towards dusk to find that the barges had withdrawn and there was nothing for it but to bivouac on the beach for the night. The Colonel seemed obsessed with the idea of a Japanese counterattack, although the Coastwatchers' scouts had quested far and wide and reported no signs of the enemy, and ordered an alert throughout the night so that in the end no one got any sleep. The barges returned at dawn and the whole party returned to base camp. The Japanese had lost over one hundred killed and the Parachute Battalion had four killed and thirteen wounded. The scouts carried the wounded Paratroops to the barges.

Colonel Krulak then decided that the Japanese outpost in Choiseul Bay should be attacked. Seton offered to guide the party since he knew the area well but the Colonel insisted on him remaining with him at the base camp. Several of the scouts were sent with the party to Choiseul Bay but as the Paratroops could not understand 'pidgin' the information the scouts provided could not be used and the expedition was not successful. After this the Colonel sent messages back to his base indicating that there were large numbers of Japanese on the verge of attacking him and that many barges were being concentrated in their area. He considered that he had done what was required of him and asked permission to withdraw. This was given.

The withdrawal had a devastating effect on the morale of the people of Choiseul. They knew nothing of the broad strategy which governed the war but saw only the immediate results. They had seen the Marine Paratroops land and had welcomed them as their saviours and now they had withdrawn leaving the Choiseul people to the Japanese. In order to bolster up their morale Lieutenant Waddell led a successful ambush party against a Japanese patrol and he and his men killed seventeen of them. The Japanese on Choiseul now began to move to certain definite centres such as Choiseul Bay and began to settle

down apparently on a permanent basis. These tactics helped the Coastwatchers who were able to watch them more easily and about the same time Flight-Lieutenant Eric Spencer, RAAF, was flown in to Choiseul to reinforce Waddell and Seton. As a result Lieutenant Waddell moved to the north west end of the island. Captain Seton kept up a roving patrol during which he attended as far as he could to the medical needs of the people and Flight-Lieutenant Spencer kept watch at the base.

The Allied strategy was to contain the Japanese on Choiseul and to harass them. Lieutenant Waddell was in demand to guide various air strikes on the Japanese positions in the Choiseul Bay area. On his return from the last of these he brought back with him Sub-Lieutenant Andressen, RANVR, to replace Flight-Lieutenant Spencer who had gone sick. He also brought in Lieutenant Robertson, AIF. Lieutenant Waddell and Captain Seton had been behind the enemy lines on Choiseul for fifteen months and had done an outstanding job. Always near to the enemy, always in danger, they had so upheld the morale of the local people that never once had they faltered in their support. The people had risked their lives and property time and time again to help not only the Coastwatchers but also the Allied forces, so much so that twenty-three airmen had been rescued and over one hundred Japanese had been killed. Between them the people of Choiseul, the scouts and Lieutenant Waddell and Captain Seton had contained, mystified and harassed well over 4,000 Japanese for the loss of one scout killed in action. There could be no better example than this of why the Japanese failed in their campaign in the Solomons and it was in the knowledge of a good job well done that Lieutenant Waddell and Captain Seton handed over their coastwatching post and went on leave.

In October 1943, after three months of most strenuous fighting, the Allied Pacific Forces were in command of the Central Solomons and in a position to begin their attack on the Northern Solomons. The operation had been undertaken to secure bases for Allied air power and from these to mount the attack on Rabaul which was the key to the Japanese positions in the South Pacific. The destruction or neutralising of enemy forces in the Central Solomons and the wiping out of their supply routes had been second in importance to that objective.

The fighting in the Solomons had also drawn into it so much of the Japanese forces and materials that it had become impossible for General Imamura and Admiral Kusaka to group their forces with a view to making strong counter attacks elsewhere in the South Pacific areas. The fall of Munda, Barakoma, Lae and Salamaua and the defeat of Japanese forces in the North Pacific during the same period forced the Imperial General Staff in Tokyo to realise that Rabaul was no longer going to be effective as a position from which either to counterattack or to bottle up Allied forces laying siege to it, and towards the end of September the Japanese began to shorten the front line of their defences in the Pacific from a line running – Aleutians – Wake Island – Marshalls – Gilberts – Nauru – Ocean Island – Bismarck Islands – northern New Guinea – Timor – Java – Sumatra – Nicobar – Andamans; to a line running through the Kuriles – Marianas – Carolines – north west New Guinea – Timor – Java – Sumatra. However, local Japanese commanders in areas which had, in theory, been abandoned, seldom followed a policy of withdrawal and in some cases major departures were made from the policy; for instance Admiral Koga, in late November 1943, sent carrier planes from Truk to Rabaul. Instances such as these must have caused considerable logistic confusion in the enemy command.

Manning a beach position

There were several more immediate and beneficial effects arising from the Central Solomons campaign. First and foremost were the tremendous losses inflicted on the enemy compared with those suffered by the Allies. The Allies lost approximately 1,850 men killed and wounded while the Japanese lost at least 10,000 men both in the fighting and by drowning as their ships were sunk when trying to reinforce their forward areas. In material too the Japanese losses were critical. At least 19 warships and 782 planes were lost compared with the Allied losses of 8 ships and 141 aircraft; in addition the Allies had behind them a tremendous industrial organisation capable of providing replacements quickly while the Japanese were short of material in their homeland and their forces were at the far end of extremely attenuated lines of supply which were very vulnerable to attack.

The Allied forces learned from experience that they had to cooperate with one another if victory was to be won. It has to be remembered in this connection that the campaign which began with Guadalcanal was the first fighting done by American forces in the second world war, and at first their procedures and techniques were rusty and uncoordinated. Bitter experience showed them that inter-service rivalry led nowhere and this lesson was brought home to them particularly strongly in New Georgia. As a result their subsequent operations were pursued to much better effect both in the use of tactical forces and economy of men and material.

Another point which became very clear during the fighting was the effect of the different attitude of mind prevailing amongst the Japanese and the Allies. The Japanese consistently underestimated the numbers of the Allied Forces and once in action their planning was inelastic. If, for example, one of their units was held up in its advance, the commanding officer would not alter his plans to meet the altered situation but would persist in his original plan even if it meant that

The final farewell to fallen comrades, Munda, New Georgia

his force was annihilated or completely neutralised. On the other hand the Allies, after the fighting on Guadalcanal, had realised that the Japanese were an extremely stubborn foe and took care to attack with an overwhelming preponderance of weapons and men. Their commanding officers from the highest to the lowest were flexible in their attitudes and would not hesitate to alter plans to suit new situations.

However, the Japanese, with far fewer men and resources and support from the air which was far from effective, put up an excellent defence of their positions in the Solomons. Their troops were seasoned men as compared with the Army units amongst the Allied forces for whom the New Georgia campaign was the first fighting most of them had ever seen, and their morale at the beginning of the fighting was high. The Marines who had been opposed to them on Guadalcanal were represented in the Central Solomons by the Raider Regiment and defence and support troops so that the brunt of the fighting fell on inexperienced army units; and this was reflected in the way that General Sasaki's men held them up, for his small forces contained the advance of three reinforced and strongly supported US Divisions (the 25th, 37th and 43rd Infantry Division supported by the 3rd New Zealand Division, 1st Marine Raider Regiment and the 4th, 9th, 10th and 11th Defence Battalions of the Fleet Marine Force together with other units). General Sasaki also managed to evacuate the majority of his troops when his positions could be held no longer and thus they were available to fight again.

From the Allied point of view a lack of training and the acceptance of the fact that war requires an attitude of mind in which the luxuries of base camps should be forgotten, were factors which took some time to learn and these, coupled with inadequacies and inefficiencies on occasion, lengthened the campaign unnecessarily. But the lessons were well learned and in Bougainville and in succeeding battles the Allied forces applied them successfully.

Bibliography

Halsey's Story Admiral W Halsey and Lt Commander J Bryan (McGraw & Hill, New York)
The Battle for the Pacific Captain Donald MacIntyre (Batsford, New York)
Reminiscences General Douglas MacArthur (McGraw & Hill, New York)
Cartwheel: Isolation of Rabaul John Miller (Government Printing Office, Washington)
Bougainville and the Northern Solomons Major John N Rentz (US Marine Corps, Washington)